CRUSADER
VS
M13/40

North Africa 1941–42

DAVID GREENTREE

OSPREY PUBLISHING
Bloomsbury Publishing Plc
Kemp House, Chawley Park, Cumnor Hill, Oxford OX2 9PH, UK
29 Earlsfort Terrace, Dublin 2, Ireland
1385 Broadway, 5th Floor, New York, NY 10018, USA
E-mail: info@ospreypublishing.com
www.ospreypublishing.com

OSPREY is a trademark of Osprey Publishing Ltd

First published in Great Britain in 2024

© Osprey Publishing Ltd, 2024

All rights reserved. No part of this publication may be reproduced or
transmitted in any form or by any means, electronic or mechanical, including
photocopying, recording, or any information storage or retrieval system,
without prior permission in writing from the publishers.

A catalogue record for this book is available from the British Library.

ISBN: PB 9781472861092; eBook 9781472861108;
ePDF 9781472861115; XML 9781472861122

24 25 26 27 28   10 9 8 7 6 5 4 3 2 1

Three-views and ammunition illustrations by Alan Gilliland
Battlescenes, cover artwork and target views by Johnny Shumate
Maps by bounford.com
Index by Rob Munro
Typeset by PDQ Digital Media Solutions, Bungay, UK
Printed and bound in India by Replika Press Private Ltd.

Osprey Publishing supports the Woodland Trust, the UK's leading woodland
conservation charity.

To find out more about our authors and books visit
www.ospreypublishing.com. Here you will find extracts, author interviews,
details of forthcoming events and the option to sign up for our newsletter.

Author's acknowledgements
I am grateful to Alan Gilliland and Johnny Shumate for helping with changes
to the artwork illustrating the book. Thanks also go to Philippa Gordon Duff
and Celia Lorimer, the daughters of Major Stuart Pitman. Last but not least,
Sofia Smith generously assisted with translations of Italian works.

Editor's note
All degree measurements relating to armour are degrees from vertical.

Title-page photograph: A Crusader I moves past Italian prisoners of war. A single
set of stowage bins on the mudguards and the absence of fuel drums on the back
suggest this is an early model. The commander and loader sit on the open hatch
lid. Early-model Crusader Is sent out to North Africa to equip 6 RTR, the first
of which disembarked during May 1941, had many notable differences from
later models. The headlight was positioned on the hull, the gun mantlet had an
open-style look and no auxiliary fuel tank was attached to the back of the hull;
nor was a stowage bin attached to the back of the turret. Additionally, a single set
of stowage bins were placed on the mudguards and half-length sand shields were
on top of the tracks. (The Tank Museum 2260-D4)

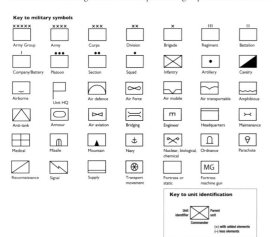

CONTENTS

INTRODUCTION

On 19 November 1941, the Crusader crews of Lieutenant-Colonel Charles Birley's 2nd Royal Gloucestershire Hussars (2 RGH) had recently arrived in Egypt following a long sea voyage from England. After completing a hurried familiarization with the desert conditions, they were brought up to the front line to participate in Operation *Crusader*, an Allied offensive intended to lift the Axis siege of the port city of Tobruk. This operation had commenced on 18 November 1941. Ordered to conduct a wide sweeping manoeuvre to get astride the supply lines of German and Italian forces blockading Tobruk, the British tankers of 22 Armoured Brigade, 2 RGH's parent formation, would encounter the M13/40 medium tanks of the 132ª Divisione corazzata 'Ariete', the Italian armoured division Benito Mussolini had committed to North Africa. The British did not think their opponents would amount to significant opposition.

By the end of 19 November, any such thoughts would be dismissed. On that morning, the Crusaders raced towards Italian infantry positions, most of which had been hastily dug near Bir el Gobi. Soon the first M13/40s could be seen, whirling up a cloud of sand that enabled the Crusaders to approach without suffering heavy losses. Serving in H Sqn, 2nd Lieutenant Geoffrey Gordon-Creed was tasked with dealing with them. A track on his Crusader was shot off during the engagement, yet he and his crew fought on, circling on the tank's other track, with the Italian tanks rapidly closing. This caused his tank to be obscured temporarily by a wall of sand. When it dispersed, two M13/40s had got to within 50m; he managed to hit both before baling out. He noticed his squadron had lost four Crusaders in a matter of minutes. The Italian tank squadron sent ahead of the main line of infantry positions had also suffered badly.

When the British effort got going again, Axis guns, emplaced among some lorries, engaged the Crusaders and inflicted additional losses. Some Italians wanted to surrender, but the British had no supporting infantry to accept prisoners. A larger tank

Knocked-out first-batch M13/40s, February 1941. In October 1940, the M13/40-equipped III Battaglione carri, part of the 32° Reggimento fanteria carrista, was sent to North Africa. The III Battaglione carri had two companies, each with 16 tanks, plus a command tank and four extra in reserve. The V Battaglione carri followed the next month, then the VI Battaglione carri, disembarking during late January 1941. Enough M13/40s were also sent to equip the XXI Battaglione carri, which had lost its tankettes at Tobruk. Most M13/40s would be lost during the British offensive conducted during December 1940 and January 1941. (The Tank Museum 6584-F2)

battle then developed as the Italians committed further M13/40s to the fight. By the end of the day, 2 RGH would be able to field only one squadron's worth of Crusaders.

The effectiveness of the M13/40s was quite a surprise to the British. Although Italy had built substantial numbers of tanks during the 1930s, most were light tankettes armed with machine guns, suitable only for operations supporting infantry through difficult mountainous terrain. During June and July 1937, two armoured brigades were organized, each including one battalion of L3/35 tankettes and two of World War I-era Fiat 3000 light tanks. Only in May 1938 did the Italian Army's general staff specify the need for three medium-tank battalions and a heavy battalion within the armoured division's table of organization – though by December 1938, when the 2° Reggimento fanteria carrista was redesignated the 32° Reggimento fanteria carrista, medium tanks did not yet exist in Italian service. In June 1940, when Italy entered World War II, the Italian Army had 1,400 light tankettes and only 96 M11/39 medium tanks, equipped with a 37mm gun. The M11/39 was soon superseded by a medium tank equipped with a 47mm gun, the M13/40, though production was limited to 250 by the end of 1940. The first batch of 400 M13/40s was supposed to have been completed by August. Hampered by a lack of radio equipment, these early-production M13/40s would be hurriedly sent to North Africa.

British infantryman inspect a knocked-out M14/41 tank after the battle of El Alamein, 24 November 1942. The lack of armour on the back of the turret suggests this tank was targeted while withdrawing from the battle. The small size is noticeable with the infantry easily clambering on it. (Associated Press/Alamy Stock Photo)

Early-production Crusader I tanks, probably from 22 Armoured Brigade, in motion during Operation *Crusader*. Note the distinctive semi-internal mantlet and the full-length sand shields on the mudguards. (The Tank Museum 2260-D6)

The M13/40 and the slightly improved M14/41 would be the mainstay of the Italian Army's armoured force from February 1941. They were on a par with the British Mk I (A9), Mk II (A10) and Mk III and Mk IV (A13) 'cruiser' tanks; these equipped most British Army armoured units until mid-1941, when the first Mk VI (A15) Crusaders appeared. The M13/40's 47mm gun could fire both armour-piercing and high-explosive rounds, while the 2-pdr gun on the British cruisers had armour-piercing ammunition only. The 47mm armour-piercing round weighed 1.44kg compared to 1.08kg for the 2-pdr round. The armour thickness of both the M13/40 and M14/41 was better than most of the early cruisers, though the Crusader had slightly thicker armour. The Italian armour plates were also brittle because of production methods; this meant the armour could split when hit.

Though the reliability of the Italian armour plates was a concern, the M13/40's engine was better than the Crusader's, which was prone to shaking and leaking oil; additionally, the British tank's water pump was defective, and tracks could be thrown. A British report compiled in July 1943 wrote about the Italian Semovente 75/18 self-propelled gun's power plant (basically the same as the engine used by the M13/40 and M14/41) and described the design, layout and construction as exemplifying sound and practical engineering. It was compact, with parts needing frequent attention easy to access.

The Crusader I could not dominate the battlefield when confronted with the M13/40, and neither would the British Army's US-supplied M3 Stuart light tank; instead, this would be accomplished by the M3 Grant and M4 Sherman medium tanks, equipping units by May and October 1942 respectively. By mid-1942, Crusaders had thicker armour, though not until the 2-pdr gun was supplanted by the 6-pdr gun could the Crusader dispatch the M13/40 and M14/41. By October 1942, the Crusader III, along with earlier models of Crusaders, equipped one squadron of each armoured regiment. The Italians would not be able to deploy a better model of medium tank until mid-1943, by which time the fighting in North Africa had ended.

CHRONOLOGY

1937

13 December — Ansaldo of Genoa is ordered to design a 47mm-gun-armed medium tank; this becomes the M13/40.

1939

27 June — The British authorities order 100 Cruiser Mk VI (A15) medium tanks without having assessed a prototype. By September the order is increased to 201.

October — The M13/40 prototype is tested.

1940

10 June — Italy enters World War II.

August — The first batch of 100 M13/40s is delivered to Italian Army units.

16 September — Italian forces reach Sidi Barrani.

October — The first M13/40s are sent to North Africa; production of the second batch of 200, some fitted with radios, begins.

October — The Crusader I production model is tested at Lulworth, Dorset.

8 December — The British Western Defence Force launches Operation *Compass*.

1941

10 February — Rommel and the first units of the Deutsches Afrikakorps deploy.

March–April — Axis forces besiege Tobruk.

April — Production of the third batch of 410 M13/40s commences. By summer 1941, a new variant with a different engine, the M14/41, is adopted. By 31 December, 376 M14/41s have been produced.

May — The first Crusader Is are sent to Egypt.

June — Launch of Operation *Battleaxe*, intended to lift the siege of Tobruk. The first Crusader Is are deployed with 2 RTR and 6 RTR.

July — The Cruiser Mk VIA, aka Crusader II, enters production. By 31 December, 250 Crusader Is and 407 Crusader IIs are produced.

September — The 'Ariete' Armoured Division completes the organization of the 132° Reggimento fanteria carrista, equipped with M13/40s.

October — A 6-pdr-armed Crusader is tested.

18 November — Operation *Crusader* commences. On 19 November, tanks of the 'Ariete' Armoured Division defeat 22 Armoured Brigade's Crusader Is at Bir el Gobi.

1942

January–February — Rommel's counter-offensive pushes the Allies to the Gazala Line.

May — The Crusader III enters production. By 31 December, 946 have been produced as well as 1,405 Crusader IIs in 1942.

26 May–21 June — The battle of Gazala sees the Axis forces gain the upper hand.

20 June — Tobruk surrenders to Axis forces.

1–27 July — The First Battle of El Alamein.

September — The 131ᵃ Divisione corazzata 'Centauro' sends two armoured battalions to North Africa to be incorporated by the 'Ariete' and 'Littorio' Armoured divisions.

23 October–11 November — The Second Battle of El Alamein sees the comprehensive defeat of the Axis forces and compels their withdrawal from Egypt.

DESIGN AND DEVELOPMENT

BRITISH

Commanders who could influence tank design had different opinions on the appearance of the future battlefield. In 1935, British Army doctrine stated that tanks could be used either for infantry-support operations (heavy tanks) or mobile assaults (medium tanks for attacking, light tanks for exploitation and scouting). A British commitment to send an expeditionary force to France was not confirmed by February 1939, further muddling the issue. Instead of developing a single tank design (easier to modify compared to multiple designs) that balanced firepower, armour protection and mobility, the British opted to design and build a variety of tank types to accommodate these different opinions. The development of multiple designs complicated production, however. Moreover, the mechanization of the British Army's cavalry along with the motorization of infantry and artillery units was prioritized over the expansion of the tank force, thus limiting funding for the development and production of medium tanks. The cavalry received light tanks, which had a proven design, because these appeared to suit the ethos of such units. The need also to build both infantry-support tanks and medium tanks limited the capacity to produce sufficient quantities of each, especially as only the government-owned Royal Carriage Factory and Carden-Loyd, owned by Vickers, could manufacture tanks. By 1937 design and manufacture would begin at two other facilities.

Italians look around a battle-damaged Cruiser Mk I (A9). The cruiser tanks ordered in 1936 would replace the old Vickers medium tanks, though they needed to be lighter to allow them to be used for exploitation and pursuit operations. The Cruiser Mk I was the first tank to possess power traverse for its turret, but the 3-pdr gun that was going to be mounted was replaced by a 2-pdr when the tank entered production in 1937. Armour was not sloped and only 14mm thick. A coaxial Vickers machine gun in the turret was complemented by two other Vickers machine guns in two small turrets on the hull. A total of 76 Cruiser Mk Is were produced in 1939 with a further 49 during 1940; they saw service in France in 1940 and North Africa in 1940–41. The close-support variant had a 3.7in howitzer with mostly smoke rounds. The Cruiser Mk I was capable of achieving a top speed of 40km/h in theory; road range was 240km. (Bettmann Archive/Keystone/Hulton Archive/Getty Images)

Prompting the development of a succession of medium tanks, the British Army's cruiser concept emphasized speed and was intended for units to operate independently of other formations. Once infantry tanks had punched a hole in the enemy's defences, cruisers would exploit it. Designed from 1934, early cruiser designs (A9 and A10) with only 6–14mm of armour were introduced by 1939. The design of cruisers would take a different path when in 1936, Lieutenant-Colonel Giffard Le Quesne Martel, Assistant Director of Mechanization at the War Office, witnessed demonstrations of the BT light tank while visiting the Soviet Union. The BT used the Christie form of suspension on large wheels, designed by the US inventor John W. Christie. Martel urged the adoption of this form of suspension with a lightweight engine. In 1937 the first Christie tank purchased from the United States would be the basis of a larger cruiser tank. Patents and manufacturing rights would be granted to Nuffield Mechanizations and Aero Limited of Birmingham,

The close-support version of the Cruiser Mk IIA (A10), armed with a 3.7in howitzer. The Cruiser Mk II had an armour thickness of 25mm, but its top speed was only 26km/h. Main armament was the same as the Cruiser Mk I, but the coaxial Vickers machine gun was replaced by a Besa machine gun. A total of 175 Cruiser Mk IIs were built, including 30 close-support Cruiser Mk IIAs mounting the 3.7in howitzer. The tank was used in France and North Africa, with 60 being deployed in Greece in 1941. The tank was not successful because it was so slow, for which the increased thickness of armour was no compensation. (SeM/Universal Images Group via Getty Images)

tasked with armaments production. The Cruiser Mk III (A13) with Christie suspension and large wheels could travel at 48km/h; the earlier cruisers built without this form of suspension could manage only 40km/h. The Cruiser Mk IV (A13 Mk II) with 30mm-thick frontal armour (the Mk III had only 14mm of armour) would soon be built.

Then the Cruiser Mk V (A13 Mk III) with standard 30mm-thick armour or equivalent was ordered. This type had distinctive sloped armour, adopted to keep the weight low; this entailed a low silhouette. The frontal armour needed was then specified by the War Office as 40mm or the equivalent. Because war was imminent by the spring of 1939, an order for 100 was placed straight off the drawing board. The War Office thought any faults could be addressed while the model was in production. At first, the tank was going to be welded, though by October because of a concern about the lack of skilled welders it was decided that it would be riveted instead. Trials conducted at Farnborough on 21 May 1940 saw the tank attain a speed of 59.5km/h. The engine compartment had no room for radiators, however, because the wide, low-profile engine designed by Henry Meadows Ltd of Wolverhampton to lower the silhouette occupied the space. The radiators were placed at the front, alongside the driver's compartment, but could not do the job they were supposed to. The resulting engine-cooling problems made the Mk V unsuitable for the desert and it would not see combat.

Nuffield did not want to join production of the tank. His company had designed its own version and this was adopted as the Cruiser Mk VI (A15) Crusader. On 13 April 1939, the War Office agreed that the Crusader would accompany the Mk V into production. The Crusader was understood to be a heavy cruiser, chosen because many of its components, tracks and suspension units would be identical to those of the Cruiser Mk III (A13). The engine was a 340hp (250kW) Nuffield Liberty 27-litre V-12 that ran on petrol. Operational range was 322km on roads, or 235km offroad. Armour was up to 40mm thick and resulted in a heavier tank that travelled at slower speeds (42km/h on roads and 24km/h offroad) compared to the Mk III. The Crusader had five rather than four road wheels on each side. Like the other cruisers, the main armament was a 2-pdr gun with a coaxial Besa machine gun. The hull was narrow and cramped and could not accommodate a machine-gunner, so the second Besa was located in a small auxiliary turret on the left of the front hull, often unmanned because the space was awkward to use. On 27 June an order for 100 was placed straight off the drawing board, subsequently increased to 201 by September 1939.

The commander at the back of the turret was close to the radio. On his left ahead of him was the gunner, usually standing to aim the gun accurately, who had to use his body strength to operate the elevating arm with his shoulder. The gunner used manual rather than geared elevation because gunnery while in motion was the norm. The loader, sitting on the ammunition bin to the commander's right, also operated the smoke discharger.

The auxiliary turret could traverse 150 degrees by hand. The machine-gunner could enter the auxiliary turret through a small hinged lid, though this method of entry was impractical and mostly not used. The auxiliary turret could be removed, though this was not always done.

CRUSADER I

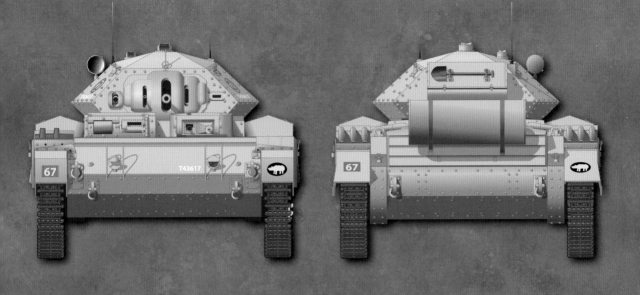

This Crusader I armed with a 2-pdr gun belongs to C Sqn, 10 Hussars, 2 Armoured Brigade, and has a sand paint scheme. The blue colour of the circle denotes the unit is the junior regiment within the brigade. A red colour would mean senior, a yellow colour the second regiment. The circle means the Crusader belongs to C Sqn. The '2' within the circle denotes No. 2 Platoon; this number was not always painted on. A triangle denoted A Sqn; a square, B Sqn; and HQ Sqn used a diamond. The unit designation on the front right and back left fender is '67' on a red background. The divisional symbol is a rhino. The T number is the production number, unique to this Crusader.

11

This Crusader III has a two-tone camouflage scheme. The commander or gunner has his head poking out of the hatch, with both of the hatch doors open. Some additional track links are attached to the hull front to improve the tank's protection. Two antennae for the No. 19 wireless radio, one HF and the other VHF, can be seen. (Military Images/ Alamy Stock Photo)

The engine had cast-iron cylinders bolted on, meaning connections could loosen, leading to oil leaks. Fuel tanks were fitted either side of the engine. Radiators drew air through louvres on the engine deck. Two cooling fans in the rear engine bulkhead were driven by the crankshaft and geared to turn at double the engine speed. This would cause problems in the desert. An engine-driven pump supplied compressed air for steering. The turret power traverse used hydraulics.

About 250 Crusader Is were produced before an up-armoured design, the Crusader Mk VIA, aka the Crusader II, was built. The thickness of armour on the turret front was increased by 10mm, and by 3–4mm on the sides and top, which meant that the lower corners of the front plate were slightly bevelled. The Crusader IIs were sent out as early as the late summer of 1941, though only by early 1942 would they be the majority in the field.

By October 1941, Nuffield had managed to place a 6-pdr gun within a slightly longer and higher new turret. The design was the Crusader III, with armour thickness set at 50mm standard. The front plate on the turret was vertical and the main gun's aperture had no external mantlet. A coaxial machine gun was placed by the 6-pdr gun and smoke dischargers could be fired through an aperture in the turret roof. A power-operated extractor fan was used to deal with the fumes created by firing the machine gun. The hatch was different, with two doors opening outward from the middle. Through the right hatch the commander had a periscope; two more periscopes were positioned further forward. The observation blocks were deleted and the openings were used for pistols. The main difference compared to the 2-pdr-armed Crusader was the absence of a loader; the commander had to carry out this role and the gunner operated the radio. The gunner/radio operator was located on the left and the commander/loader on the right. Stowage space for the new ammunition was the main concern, thus the need to free up space by omitting the loader. A Bren gun and a submachine gun were also stored within the turret. Range with the 500-litre tank was 177km. The auxiliary fuel tank held 136 litres. The Mk IV Liberty engine had updated water pumps along with a shaft drive to turn the cooling fans. Top speed was 43km/h on roads and 24km/h offroad.

ITALIAN

The design and production of a medium tank took a great deal of time and was not a priority for the Italians, who instead concentrated on producing light tankettes. The Fiat 3000 was the first Italian light tank to be produced and the Mod. 21 equipped with two 6.5mm machine guns entered service by 1921. By 1927, a tank regiment was formed with 100 Fiat 3000s. The tankette was designated L5/21 by the time Italy entered World War II on 10 June 1940. The Mod. 30, a medium tank based on this design with a 37mm gun and 30mm armour, entered service by 1930, and was subsequently designated the L5/30. Few would be built, however, with only 48 delivered to the Italian Army. In 1940, the 'Centauro' and 'Littorio' Armoured divisions would each equip two battalions mostly with L5/21s plus some L5/30s. By 1941 these types were sent to training units.

The Italians designed and manufactured other light tankettes, based on the fast and cheap British Carden-Loyd Mk VI design. Fiat acquired the licence and the first Italian design was the CV-33 (later redesignated the L3/33), followed by the CV-35 (L3/35) and CV-38 (L3/38). Ansaldo of Genoa would also manufacture them. Weighing 3.2 tonnes and protected by 14mm of frontal armour, the CV-33, of which 300 were produced, had a single 6.5mm machine gun. From early 1935 the first of 2,200 CV-35s with twin 8mm machine guns were produced; 595 were used by the Italians during the conquest of Ethiopia in 1935–37. Few examples of the L3/33 and L3/35 continued in front-line service after 1941 because their armour was vulnerable to the British anti-tank rifle.

Only 96 examples of the M11/39 medium tank equipping two battalions had been completed by May 1940. Fiat made the engines and transmissions, with Ansaldo completing the assembly. The 37mm gun was not in the turret; instead, it occupied a fixed position within the hull with only a 30-degree traverse because space was limited. Twin 8mm machine guns housed within the turret could be operated by the commander. The frontal armour thickness of 30mm was insufficient, however, being

An M11/39 medium tank, c.1940. This tank is the second tank of the second platoon. Company designation is not possible to ascertain because the colour of the unit symbol is unclear. The hull-mounted 37mm gun was a major disadvantage when facing tanks with the main gun in a turret. (Keystone/Getty Images)

This early M13/40 can be identified as being from the first production batch by its full-length fenders and the absence of a radio aerial. Throughout the war in North Africa, the main issue the Axis armies faced was keeping the force supplied. Sea routes from mainland Europe to North Africa were interdicted by Allied submarines and aircraft, many based on Malta. In particular, the sinking of oil tankers hampered Rommel's ability to exploit his armour's mobility, sometimes at crucial moments. Additionally, supplies had to be disembarked at ports with proper working facilities and then transported by lorry. The 'Ariete' Armoured Division's supply system was good, though getting enough oil was problematic. Bowsers and lorries had to offload the oil from the tankers at Tripoli or Benghazi. The logistics base aimed to stock enough material so 'Ariete' could fight for five days without external resupply; but supplies had to travel along the coast road and could be interdicted by aircraft. The lorries used the hours of darkness to negate such attacks. The distance from Tripoli to Benghazi was 1,030km, and from Tripoli to El Alamein 1,800km. A total of 70,000–150,000 tonnes of supplies were needed per month to supply the Axis forces. At a distance of 1,030km 'Ariete' needed 500 lorryloads per day. Lorries needed an entire day to make the journey as a speed of only 48km/h could be maintained. The use of trailers and captured lorries mitigated the problems, but the maintenance of so many types of lorry was an issue. (The Tank Museum 3803-B6)

incapable of withstanding hits from the British 2-pdr gun. The three-man crew had no intercom. Production ceased by the middle of 1940, by which time only 100 M11/39s had been built.

A 37mm gun with restricted traverse was of limited utility in a tank battle. Placing a larger gun, the 47mm, in the turret was the priority and Ansaldo received the order for a new 13-tonne tank on 13 December 1937. The tank's speed needed to be at least 35km/h and sufficient fuel had to be carried for 12 hours' driving. The main gun would be a licensed copy of the Austrian Böhler 47mm M35 anti-tank gun, with a coaxial 8mm Breda 38 machine gun. Two bow-mounted machine guns were to be located in the hull. The resulting M13/40 was designed in 1938, with the first prototype being built in October 1939. The design was accepted, despite the tank weighing 14 tonnes fully loaded because of its thicker armour. The first 100 M13/40s were produced by Ansaldo by June 1940 and entered service by August. None of the initial batch had radios. The tank had a 105hp (77kW) eight-cylinder SPA 8T diesel engine. Top speed was 32km/h on roads and 13km/h offroad. Range was 200km on roads and 120km offroad.

The first batch, of 100 tanks, had fenders along the length of the tank. The second batch, of 200 tanks and completed by the autumn of 1940, had fenders only at the front of the tank. Considering the M13/40 fought in the desert this did not make much sense. The jack formerly on the left front fender on the first 100 M13/40s now occupied a position on the left rear, a position where a set of spare road wheels used to sit, meaning only a single set of spare road wheels was on the right rear of the tank. Also, a new foldable seat for the commander/gunner was added, meaning 17 fewer 47mm rounds could be stored in the fighting compartment. Some of this batch were fitted with radios. The third batch of M13/40s – 410 in number, produced from spring 1941 – were built with a modified radiator filler cap, and included a ventilator with a radiator for engine-oil cooling. The power of the SPA 8T engine was increased to 125hp (92kW), with the exhausts having to be altered because of the new motor.

M13/40

Built during spring 1941, this late-production M13/40 is from the VIII Battaglione carri, 132° Reggimento fanteria carrista. Tactical tank symbols assisted identification of tanks within the battalion. The first company had the colour red, the second company blue, the third company yellow and the fourth company green. These rectangles had 1–4 white bars denoting the platoon; company command tanks' insignia had no bars. Battalion command tanks bore a black rectangle. Some tanks bore the rectangular symbol on the hatch to the fighting compartment. On this example, unit insignia on the back plates of the fighting compartment includes '132' on the back left and the battalion designation on the back right. A blue symbol on the turret denotes the 2ª Compagnia; the solid colour (with no stripes) denotes the company commander's vehicle. The registration plates on the front and back are unique to this vehicle.

Italian personnel inspect an early-production M13/40 medium tank. This is a first-batch M13/40 with a machine gun used for air defence mounted ahead of the turret hatch. (agefotostock/ Alamy Stock Photo)

Production of the M14/41 medium tank commenced during the summer of 1941. Installation of a new engine, the eight-cylinder SPA 15T M41, increased speed to 33km/h on roads and 16km/h offroad; the new engine was adopted by the 80th tank to be produced in the series. The cooling system and exhaust pipes had a different appearance; and fenders once again ran along the tank's length. By the end of 1941, with 376 M14/41s produced concurrently with 170 M13/40s, production of the latter ceased. The M14/41 was by then operational with the 'Littorio' Armoured Division. Other M14/41 modifications would include X-shaped stamping on the fenders to strengthen them, and the addition of mud scrapers near the drive-sprocket wheels. The last models had drum supports, four at the back and two on the right side. The M14/41 remained in production until late 1942.

The Germans had let the Italians produce a PzKpfw III medium tank, though without armament or gun sights; these parts would be supplied by Germany. The Italian Army general staff did not want to rely on German industry, however, and did not accept the offer. This discussion took place during August 1941, when a copy of the Crusader was also being built by the Italians. Problems with the suspension delayed completion of a prototype until the spring of 1942, however, and by the time trials had been concluded the campaign in the desert was over. Instead, the M15/42, armed with a 47/40 gun capable of firing the new EP (*effetto pronto*, 'ready effect') hollow-charge round would be built. A new 190hp (140kW) engine made speeds of 38km/h on roads possible, with a range of 220km on roads and 130km offroad. An order for 280 M15/42s was placed in October 1942.

The M15/42 had 50mm of frontal armour and 25mm of side armour. Its 47mm gun was capable of firing a hollow-charge round. Some 200 M15/42s would be produced up to September 1943, but the only combat they would see was against the Germans in Rome. Most would be used by the Germans. (Totorvdr59/Wikimedia/CC BY-SA 4.0)

Both the M13/40 and M14/41 had command variants. The *carro centro radio* (radio centre tank) was produced from early 1941 by fitting a second radio set, the Marelli RF 2 CA with a range of 8km when the tank was in motion, or 20–30km when the tank was stationary. Each command tank had two aerials. By October 1941, ten M13/40 and two M14/41 command tanks operated with the units, with another 13 M14/41s being built.

The M13/40's hull had an engine compartment at the back and a fighting compartment to the front. The engine compartment had two diesel fuel tanks, and the engine with fans and radiators. The fighting compartment housed the crew of four, ammunition racks initially for 70 rounds, the radio and two 8mm Breda 38 machine guns. Another machine gun was stored on a rack on the right of the fighting compartment to be attached to a mounting on the turret roof and used against aircraft. The turret housed the 47/32 Mod. 1935 gun, a coaxial machine gun, a scope elevator and two panoramic scopes. Circular ammunition bins in the turret housed 34 rounds for immediate use.

The gunner and driver used an entrance on the left side of the hull. This could be left partially open by means of a stay. The commander and gunner used a turret hatch closed by two doors hinged on either side. Two hatches on the engine chamber attached by a central hinge could be closed from both the outside and inside.

The M14/41 was almost identical to the M13/40. The mounting for the twin Breda machine guns differed, however, and the track guards extended along the length of the tank. The first unit to be deployed with the M14/41 was the 'Littorio' Armoured Division's X Battaglione carri, placed under command of the 'Ariete' Armoured Division. The tanks of the XII Battaglione carri were lost when the transport ship taking them to North Africa was sunk. A total of 710 M13/40s and 730 M14/41s, including command tanks, were produced.

TECHNICAL SPECIFICATIONS

FIREPOWER

Crusader

The 2-pdr gun's firing mechanism was heavy and with free elevation, not geared; an arrangement not conducive to accuracy. The Axis tanks had geared elevation for their guns, allowing steadier aiming while stationary. The 2-pdr's gunner balanced the weapon with his shoulder, which helped with aiming while in motion, though firing with a trigger and not a foot pedal disturbed the gunner.

The 2-pdr armour-piercing round could penetrate 68mm of armour at 100m, 52mm at 500m, 37mm at 1,000m and 27mm at 1,500m. The 2-pdr high-velocity round could go through 75mm of armour at 100m, 58mm at 500m, 41mm at 1,000m and 30mm at 1,500m. The speed of the armour-piercing round was 792m/sec; the high-velocity round had a speed of 852m/sec. The absence of explosive fillers meant crews of enemy anti-tank guns and tanks had a high survivability rate.

The use of ammunition boxes meant 16 rather than 20 2-pdr rounds could be stored in the Crusader I/II turret. The ration boxes at the back corner of the fighting compartment were done away with; in their place, a small bin holding 12 rounds occupied the space. A single area for 79 rounds was on the left of the fighting compartment. This made a total of 107 2-pdr rounds when ammunition bins were installed, or 65 (25 high-explosive and 40 smoke) rounds of 3in ammunition on the close-support Crusader. The Crusader III could stow 76 6-pdr rounds. The Crusader

OPPOSITE

The crew of a Crusader tank clean the barrel of its 2-pdr gun, 6 February 1942. (Lieutenant J.E. Barker/Imperial War Museums via Getty Images)

I/II had 4,950 machine-gun rounds; the Crusader III 3,375 machine-gun rounds. Both had 30 2in bomb-thrower rounds.

The 37mm gun on the M3 Stuart was more effective because its round had a ballistic cap. Bemoaning the lack of ballistic caps for 2-pdr rounds, Colonel William M. Blagden, Deputy Director of Fighting Vehicles, Ministry of Supply, was sent to the War Office during the summer of 1942 to emphasize the importance of acquiring them, despite the stowage problems longer rounds would cause. These rounds could also be made with a ballistic cap on the cap, thus the term APCBC. Blagden told the War Office that 2-pdr ballistic-capped rounds should be sent out to North Africa within four months. He knew no order had been placed by early August, however; none would be sent. Testing was found wanting at home, despite the APCBC round's ability to penetrate 50mm of armour. He asked for the super-charged rounds to be sent out and this did happen.

The 6-pdr QF Mk III gun, a 57mm weapon, used armour-piercing rounds only during the campaign in the desert. The armour-piercing shot could penetrate 97mm of armour at 100m, 82mm at 500m, 66mm at 1,000m and 43mm at 2,000m. These depths of penetration increased to 104mm, 87mm, 70mm and 46mm with a high-velocity round.

The Crusader III was not operational until September 1942, however, because of a series of minor problems with its gun. A total of 60 man-hours had to be put into each tank to ensure faults in the original assembly were corrected. Blagden noted (Knight 2015: 112) that an optional geared elevation control was requested by gunners. The No. 39 sight for the 6-pdr gun had a graticule still obscuring the target at 2,500yd (2,286m). The limit to aiming was thought to be 1,000yd (914m) because of these issues (Knight 2015: 113). The lack of armoured bins made fires likely when hit. Crews did manage to bale out successfully, however. The commander was also the

The British 2-pdr HE round (above) and 6-pdr HE round (below).

The Italian 47mm APBC round (above) and HE round (below).

loader, although some units employed him as the gunner. The commander's periscope was attached to the offside turret hatch door, usually open when fighting, and he preferred to be exposed to observe his surroundings. If he was not, observation of fire was difficult and sometimes the platoon commander would stand off to the flank to watch the fall of shot.

M13/40

The M13/40 was armed with the Austrian-designed 47/32 Mod. 1935 gun, capable of firing both armour-piercing and high-explosive rounds. This gun primarily used APHE shells with a muzzle velocity of 630m/sec and high-explosive shells with a muzzle velocity of 250m/sec. The APHE shell could penetrate 52mm of armour at 100m, 41mm at 500m, 30mm at 1,000m and 22mm at 1,500m. The APBC round also used could penetrate 52mm of armour at 100m, 46mm at 500m, 39mm at 1,000m and 33mm at 1,500m.

Main-gun elevation was controlled by a 20cm-diameter handwheel to the loader's left. It was easy to get at, though not easy to operate because the mechanism was stiff and fine adjustment was difficult owing to the coarse teeth of the mechanism. The handwheel required 16.75 turns for the gun to travel the full arc of 40 degrees (-15 to +25 degrees). Rotation through 360 degrees could be achieved manually with a handwheel or by using a hydraulic system. The housing for the handwheel traverse was attached to the lower rim of the turret ring to the loader's right. A prismatic extension to the telescopic sight meant the user did not need to move his head when sighting. The height of the eyepiece could be adjusted within limits. The gun could be operated by a foot pedal or manually. Accuracy for the gun was 100 per cent at 100m, 95 per cent at 500m, 46 per cent (52 per cent for the M39) at 1,000m and 17 per cent at 1,500m. The comparable accuracy of the Crusader's 2-pdr gun was 100 per cent at 100m, 67 per cent at 500m, 26 per cent at 1,000m and 12 per cent at 1,500m (Jentz 1998: 48).

Initially, 104 47mm rounds were taken into combat, then 87 following the addition of foldable seats for the loader and commander. Of the 87 rounds carried, 34 would be stowed vertically in two curved bins in the rear of the turret; one had nine rounds, the other 25. The other 53 rounds were stowed in the fighting compartment. A spring cap was fitted on the top of each round and the base had a rubber washer to facilitate storage.

Two 8mm Breda 38 machine guns in a gimbal mounting on the right of the hull had a firing arc of 30 degrees. They could be elevated by 20 degrees and depressed by 10 degrees. A telescope was mounted between the two machine guns. A third Breda 38 was placed coaxially to the left of the main gun. A fourth Breda 38 could be mounted on the turret on a detachable bracket allowing both traverse and elevation. The bracket was mounted in a sleeve on the turret roof in front of the hatch. When not mounted this way, the machine gun and bracket would be placed on two brackets on the right wall of the fighting compartment. The tank carried 127 24-round magazines (3,048 8mm machine-gun rounds) in racks situated mostly in the fighting compartment.

PROTECTION

Crusader

On the Crusader I, the front glacis on the hull was sloped, but the back and sides were vertical. Crusaders had a sloped turret with no cupola, designed to give the crew sufficient internal space. The 40mm sloped frontal armour was intended to protect against most tanks at the time armed with a 37mm gun. The hull side armour was only 14mm thick, though the turret side armour was 19mm thick and set at 50 degrees. Crusaders had 13mm-thick armour panels attached to the hull sides – a permanent factory-installed addition with the Crusader IIs – to protect against the 5cm gun arming the PzKpfw III. Crusader IIs also had 49mm of armour on the front glacis and mantlet.

The cruiser tank was built for speed and was not an infantry-support tank, hence it had thinner armour. By contrast the Matilda II, an infantry-support tank, had armour of up to 78mm thickness on the front. A PzKpfw III Ausf. G, armed with a 3.7cm and then a 5cm gun, had 30mm-thick armour on the front and sides, while the Ausf. H had 60mm of armour on the hull front, 35mm on the gun mantlet and 30mm of side armour. Both German types were deployed to North Africa during 1941.

The Italian Army tested the 47/32 Mod. 1935 gun on armour sloped at 30 degrees. This testing saw the Mod. 1935 APHE round penetrate 55mm of armour at a range of 91m, 43mm at 457m and 32mm at 914m. The Italians determined that a Mod. 1935 round could not penetrate the Crusader I's gun mantlet, but could penetrate the turret front at 640m, and hull front at 914m. The round could go through the Crusader I's turret side at 640m and hull side at 1,100m (Jentz 1998: 55).

The Crusader III had 32mm of armour on the vertical turret front and 51mm on the mantlet. The hull front had 32mm of armour at 60 degrees, making it the equivalent of 52mm thickness. The hull sides and rear had 27mm of armour at 90 degrees, with the turret side armour angled to be the equivalent of 39.7mm thickness.

In Blagden's opinion, by mid-1942 Crusader squadrons were used for reconnaissance or kept in reserve because their armament and armour were deficient compared to those of the Sherman (Knight 2015: 115). This was not the experience of the tankers themselves, however, as no fewer than 94 Crusaders (including 34 armed with the 6-pdr gun) were battle casualties during the Second Battle of El Alamein. This compared to 53 Grants and 87 Shermans. Major-General Charles W. Norman, who replaced Major-General Richard L. McCreery as Chief of Staff, Middle East Command, in September 1942, explained that the Crusader squadron would be detached from the regiment during operations; their speed meant they could re-join the regiment when required (Knight 2015: 116). The Crusader's low silhouette meant that their commanders positioned the tanks in shallow depressions to get close to the enemy.

A technician tests a Crusader tank before sending it to the Royal Armoured Corps, 13 December 1941. (Bert Hardy/Picture Post/Hulton Archive/Getty Images)

Rommel stands with binoculars near an M13/40. The rivets securing the armour plates are evident. (The Tank Museum 3182-B2)

M13/40

The M13/40 had an armour thickness of 40mm on the turret front at 16 degrees and 30mm on the hull front. The hull front glacis had 25mm of armour at 81 degrees. The turret sides and back had 25mm, at 22 degrees, while the gun mantlet had 33mm. The hull sides and back had 25mm. The engine top and lower cover plates had 10mm and 9mm of armour respectively. The turret top plate had 14mm at 85 degrees and the belly bottom plate had 15mm at 90 degrees. The side hatch was a weak point, with only 8mm of armour.

British tests had the 2-pdr round at 792m/sec going through the M13/40's gun-mantlet armour at a range of 549m, the turret front at 549m, the hull front at 732m and superstructure front at 1,190m. The round could go through the turret side at 1,530m and the hull and superstructure side at 1,750m. The ranges the British specified had the shot perforating armour from a side angle of 30 degrees. Also, a successful shot was defined as 80 per cent success, where four out of five shots hitting the plate would see at least one-fifth of the shot penetrating the plate with the missile intact (Jentz 1998: 46).

In an effort to improve the M13/40's protection, sandbags were often piled on the hull front, though this contributed to engine overheating and reduced the tank's speed. The armour on the tank would often split when hit because it was too brittle and bolted on.

A knocked-out M13/40. The ability of the British 2-pdr gun to penetrate the M13/40's armour is apparent. (The Tank Museum 3182-B3)

MOBILITY

Crusader

All Crusader variants had a top speed of 42km/h on roads and 24km/h offroad. Total fuel capacity with auxiliary tank was 636 litres, providing a notional operational range of 227km on roads and 105km offroad.

The Crusader was criticized for a host of mechanical defects. On 10 December 1941, Brigadier Leslie S. Lloyd, the officer at GHQ Middle East Forces in charge of AFVs, wrote to the War Office pointing out certain issues (Knight 2015: 115). He noted that leaks from oil galleries needed engine removal because the unions under the engine could not be accessed easily. Also the fans failed, water leaked, the water pump failed, and the Crusader had a tendency to burn when hit. These issues were confirmed by Lieutenant-General Martel, by now the Commander of the Royal Armoured Corps. On 2 October 1941, when the 166 Crusaders of 22 Armoured Brigade arrived in Egypt, orders stated that a local modification to the axles was required (Knight 2015: 22). On 18 October 1941, Martel noted that unit workshop facilities had to modify the axles on Crusaders because of production defects. This work, he stated, should be done at home because the unit workshops had too much other work to do. Colonel Blagden, sent to the Middle East to investigate, noticed that the axles of some batches of Crusaders mostly had only bent, however, and that this had not led to immobilization (Knight 2015: 28). The workshops had used precious man-hours carrying out pointless work on the modification to the axles. This meant time for other maintenance work was lacking and exaggerated the effects of other problems on the opinions some had about the Crusader.

Many British Army officers wrote disparagingly about the Crusader. On 14 January 1942, Major Peter T.W. Sykes of the Queen's Bays (2nd Dragoon Guards) shared his opinions, based on a march through the desert conducted by 2 Armoured Brigade

The engine of this tank, probably a Crusader II, is being worked on. Note the two-tone camouflage paint pattern. In the background, a lorry transporter is about to load a second Crusader. Between 18 November and 26 December 1941, 7th Armoured Division's workshops received 134 Crusaders, sent 39 further back to base workshops and repaired 95. These 95 had 120 different issues; 43 had either an oil or a water leak, while 38 had fan problems. Also during this time, engineers had to spend time on strengthening axles on all the Crusaders of 22 Armoured Brigade. Some of the axles had fractured, though not many. On 7 March 1942, Brigadier Lloyd, the officer at GHQ Middle East Forces in charge of AFVs, criticized the need for such work (Knight 2015: 48). (The Tank Museum 9404-C2)

A Crusader I or II with its turret hatch open and some of the sand shields removed so work can be done on the running gear. Note the Operation *Crusader* markings on the front part of the sand shield and the turret symbol denoting the squadron. Despite efforts by their crews, Crusaders could not easily be maintained in the field. By early August 1942, 296 were at base ordnance depots or base ordnance workshops; by mid-September, this number had risen to 337 and by the end of 1942, 456. The total was 335 on 24 February 1943, but this number did not include Crusader IIIs. Base workshops simply had too many to work on, though the Crusader was not the priority now that the Sherman was in service. (The Tank Museum 10414-002)

(Knight 2015: 46). During the first 100–400 miles (160–645km), nearly all the Crusaders had oil leaks, probably because of substandard assembly during the production process. Some of the leaks could only be remedied by removing tanks and radiators – an operation not possible when on the march. At 500–600 miles (805–965km), components such as water pumps, air compressors and shock absorbers had failed. By 1,200–1,500 miles (1,930–2,415km), the Crusaders were generally unreliable and in need of an overhaul. Sykes also thought the Crusader's silhouette, with large road wheels, made a good aiming point for enemy gunners.

On 4 February 1942, Lloyd wrote to the War Office, stating the Crusader was mechanically unreliable. An overhaul was necessary every 1,200 miles (1,930km); this compared to 3,500 miles (5,635km) for the M3 Stuart light tank. The effects of long approach marches through dusty environments could not be compensated for by workshop capacity. He suggested that Crusaders equipped with 2-pdr guns should not be sent out. In the meantime, problems needed to be dealt with; the tendency of the Crusader to ignite when hit was because the 2-pdr rounds were stowed around the fighting compartment with cartridge cases exposed. Lieutenant-Colonel Jocelyn A. Barlow, a staff officer sent to investigate losses during Operation *Crusader*, suggested the ammunition should be stowed in lockers. On 8 March 1942, Lloyd confirmed that splinter-proof stowage bins would be installed. He also suggested that the M3 Grants be distributed to each armoured brigade to guard the Crusaders. On 8 March a memorandum confirmed that each Crusader-equipped armoured regiment would get a squadron of Grants.

Replacing Lloyd in April 1942, Major-General Richard L. McCreery found fault with the Crusaders' performance. He was critical of 10th Royal Hussars (Prince of

Wales's Own) using up much-needed Crusader mileage, noting that they must keep 600 miles (965km) available. According to McCreery, overhauls for a Crusader required eight weeks, though he probably included some time awaiting parts in this assessment. The Stuart, he wrote, needed only four weeks. Following the battle of Gazala in May–June 1942, McCreery reported less on mechanical casualties among the Crusader force. The armoured stowage bins also helped protect crews, though new Crusaders still had problems for 150 miles (242km) when they joined the units, particularly oil leaks and water-pump issues. For example, of a batch of 16 new Crusaders, ten had oil leaks and had to be sent back to base workshops. For a time, special running-in tests of 100 miles (161km) had to be completed before the new Crusaders could be sent forward for battle. By 2 July 1942, the running-in tests were stopped; instead, base workshops conducted intensive tests and dealt with oiling system problems. A 40-mile (64km) road test was then carried out. This meant base workshops had to spend a lot of time working on newly disembarked Crusaders instead of battle casualties.

The disembarkation of Crusaders from ships and railway cars without water to cool the engine was thought to explain why so many Crusaders had issues, but this was the same as with other tanks. Perhaps factory issues were the reason why the Crusader was particularly affected by problems. A number of British companies, some new to tank production, commenced building the Crusader during 1942. The Ministry of Production admitted that volume of production was prioritized at the expense of immediate reliability.

Problems persisted despite efforts to deal with them. During July 1942, 7 Armoured Brigade Group ordnance company listed the faults with Crusaders (Knight 2015: 101–02). Of 117 Crusaders that passed through the workshops during the month, 32 had water-pump leaks and 28 main gallery oil leaks, with 26 gearbox seizures and 34 low engine-power issues leading to carburation issues and smoking exhausts. The issue of smoking exhausts made it easier for the enemy to identify the Crusaders. The sprockets did not fail as much, however, as work on hardening them had been done by then; some Crusaders of 2 Armoured Brigade tested the hardened sprockets during March 1942. Lieutenant-Colonel Baird expected them to last for 1,500 miles (2,415km), but the engine life was still only 1,400 miles (2,255km); after that, the cylinders had to be re-bored (Knight 2015: 81).

The Crusader had a range of 70–90 miles (112–145km), though when used for reconnaissance this was markedly reduced because of the amount of time spent using battery power while stationary. In Norman's view, the chief problem was reliability, though the provision of spare parts improved as the Western Desert campaign continued, with supply dumps established in forward areas (Knight 2015: 117).

M13/40

The M13/40's SPA 8T engine was a four-stroke diesel type with eight cylinders arranged four on each side at 90 degrees. The diesel engine and fuel proved to be hard to ignite, which saved the lives of many crewmen when M13/40s were hit in combat. A filter designed to keep out impurities and dust was placed at the end of the air-intake duct. The fuel for the cylinders was supplied by injection pumps, one per cylinder, grouped in a single mechanical complex controlled by the engine. The first

This photograph of an M14/41 preserved at the Museo storico dei carristi, Rome, provides a good view of the running gear and tracks. This tank bears the insignia of a 2ᵃ Compagnia command tank, as the identification symbol is a solid-blue rectangle. (Heinz Guderian/Wikimedia/CC BY-SA 3.0)

ignition was assisted by spark plugs, after which ignition happened automatically. Pumps circulated oil for lubrication and cooling was done by water cooled by fans blowing air through two radiators and circulated by a centrifugal pump. Four air filters applied to the engine filtered air before it entered the eight cylinders. The M13/40 was considered to be underpowered, with its engine much complained about; it could wear out after 500km because the filters did not work properly. In December 1941, the M13/40's inadequate cooling system, faulty batteries and high fuel consumption led Generale di brigata Mario Balotta, the commander of the 'Ariete' Armoured Division, to demand a new engine (Cappellano & Battistelli 2012: 35).

The M13/40 managed 32km/h on roads and 19km/h offroad, while the improved SPA 15T engine of the M14/41 meant it could achieve 35km/h on roads and 19km/h offroad; the added power of the engine was mitigated by the tank's additional weight, however. The M14/41 had a range of 200km on roads and about 80km offroad. The tank could carry 180 litres of fuel. The gearbox had a speed reducer, making possible the selection of four normal and four low-ratio gears. This was done with a lever connecting the secondary shaft of the gearbox with the axle.

For both the M13/40 and the M14/41, each track consisted of eight links of equal size hinged together by pins. Drive wheels at the front and idler wheels at the back caused the track to tense or loosen while resting on three rubberized guide rollers. The vehicle itself rested on four bogies, each with two pairs of rubberized rollers. The bogies were independent of each other to ensure a flexible suspension, allowing the tracks to adapt to unevenness in the terrain and keep in constant contact with the carriage rollers, eliminating a principal cause of sliding.

VISION AND COMMUNICATIONS

Crusader

The Crusader's main turret had no cupola; instead, a large hatch was lifted up by torsion bars on both ends and shifted to the back. The hatch had to be firmly secured; if not, it could swing shut of its own accord. Rotating periscopes on the turret roof were used by both the loader and the commander. A sighting periscope was used by the gunner. Two vision blocks with hinged flaps on the turret sides also helped with observation.

Early Crusaders used the No. 9 radio with a range of 13km, operating in the 1.875–5 MHz range. The No. 19 set equipping Crusaders from late 1941 was developed in 1940 by Pye Ltd of Cambridge when the War Office asked for a tactical radio for tanks after Dunkirk. The set had a High Frequency radio transmitter receiver intended for radio communications up to 80km with amplifier, as used by higher units' command tanks, plus a Very High Frequency transmitter receiver for line-of-sight use up to 1.6km. The High Frequency set operated between 2.5–6.25 MHz for the Mk I or 2–8 MHz for the Mk 2 and Mk 3; a switch enabled the operator to change rapidly between two frequencies. Morse code could be used. A 2.4–4.8m antenna gave the HF set a range of 16km for speech and 25km for Morse code when in motion. Operating between 229–241 MHz, the VHF set used a 64cm rod for the antenna system. In practice, however, speech had a range of about 500m due to the receiver's lack of sensitivity.

An intercom was also part of the radio for crewmen to talk to each other. This was essential for the crew as direct communication within the tank was not possible. A microphone/headphone assembly was provided for each crewman with snatch plugs to disconnect them quickly if the crew needed to bale out.

A good head-on shot of a Crusader I or II with the commander sitting on the open turret hatch lid and the driver visible through his hatch. This tank is leading a convoy of supply lorries; note the sand being displaced as they proceed. Crusader commanders tended to go into combat with the turret hatch open to obtain a better view. The auxiliary turret would only be done away with officially in February 1942. (The Tank Museum 5938-B2)

M13/40

The M13/40 driver had a rectangular window located on the front plate with a hatch hinged on the outside and operated from the inside by a lever capable of maintaining fully open, intermediate and closed positions while moving. When the hatch was closed a longitudinal slot was used, capable of being closed from the inside by a plate attached to the hatch. The driver could also use a low-magnification periscope incorporating two prisms: an upper prism protruding from the roof of the hull and a lower prism at the driver's level. The machine-gunner in the hull had a low-magnification telescope positioned between the two machine guns. The fighting compartment had four circular slots around the hull sides and back for vision and the use of small arms; these slots were closed by turning plates from inside the hull. The commander and loader used two panoramic telescopes for 360-degree vision and two slots on each side of the turret.

The commander could send orders to the driver by placing a lever on a kind of clock; this appeared on the driver's screen, though this system could only be used when the gun was pointing along the direction of travel because the mechanism was mounted on the hull. The commander would not be able to reach the system otherwise. An intercom system linked the other crew members to the commander with throat microphones and headsets. The commander and loader could not use the microphones if the turret was turned to the rear because they were plugged into the lower part of the carriage. The radio set, a Marelli RF 1 CA transceiver, operating in the 27.2–33.4 MHz range and with a range of 5–12km, was only standard on M13/40s produced from mid-1941. The radio was positioned to the right of the machine-gunner on the wall of the fighting compartment.

The small size of the M13/40's turret is certainly evident in this shot of a commander in full tanker's gear. (The Tank Museum 0303-D6)

28

THE COMBATANTS

BRITISH ARMOUR DOCTRINE

Severe manpower losses among British forces during World War I prompted questions about the merits of committing a large land force to continental operations. The tank's utility was discounted by many, however, because of extreme parochialism on the part of many senior British Army officers who put the interests of the various branches of service first. The British Army's infantry argued that the tank should be for infantry support and needed to be heavily armoured. The cavalry wanted a light tank for scouting and pursuit. Cavalry officers who had adopted tanks by World War II still thought charging an enemy gun line was a valid tactic. Both schools of thought sought to dominate ideas about the use of armour. Many tank theorists suggested that a tank-only armoured division was needed, with only a minority realizing the importance of a combined-arms approach. The Chief of the Imperial General Staff, the head of the British Army, did not possess enough authority to impose a solution. By 1939 no consensus on the role of tank units existed and this hampered the development of combined-arms practice.

The way exercises were conducted did not help solve the problem. An experimental mechanized force (EMF) was established during 1927 and conducted yearly exercises, though the lessons learned would not inform the organization of the next year's exercises. Instead, a different concept would be tested; but while official policy by 1924 stated that each branch of service was dependent on the cooperation of the others, many did not accept this doctrine. The armour theorist Captain Basil H. Liddell Hart saw the infantry and tank force as complementing each other, while others suggested that infantry would only occupy territory seized by the tanks and

Taken during the autumn of 1941, this photograph shows a British tanker escaping from a burning Crusader tank. (Eric Borchert/ullstein bild via Getty Images)

guard lines of communication. The 1924 doctrine, however, stated that the primary role of the tank was to facilitate the forward movement of the infantry, and commanders who saw tanks as only assisting the infantry disbanded the EMF in 1928.

Then those with influence forced through a policy that tank brigades would not need infantry within their establishment, despite the 1929 doctrine emphasizing the critical importance of close liaison between infantry and the tank force, with infantry suppressing the enemy guns to help the tanks make headway. They saw the lack of armoured carriers to enable the infantry to keep up with the tanks as the main problem; because of the lack of funds, many thought they had to take a stance on priorities. The German policy of using lorries to transport infantry was discounted.

The debate about what shape a mobile force should take would play out throughout the 1930s. A permanent tank brigade was established in 1933 and the concept of a 'mobile division' tested in 1934. Brigadier (later Major-General) Percy C.S. Hobart commanded the tank brigade, Major-General George M. Lindsay the mechanized infantry brigade. The two men argued and would not help each other; the exercise concluded that an infantry division and a cavalry brigade could defeat a mobile division. The exercise ended any prospect of a balanced combined-arms unit. The Mobile Division, formed on 24 November 1937, would focus on traditional cavalry missions such as scouting, guarding the flanks, exploitations and pursuit, and raids. Its units would only support the main attack on or close to the battlefield and not lead the attack. The Mobile Division had two mechanized cavalry brigades along with the tank brigade for this role. The tank brigade would assist the cavalry and probably would not fight independently. The cruisers with which it was equipped would suit the mobile assault. The speed of mobile assaults would mean support from other arms would not be possible.

Commanded by Major-General Roger Evans, 1st Armoured Division, as the Mobile Division was redesignated in April 1939, deployed to mainland Europe by May 1940, after the German attack on France had begun. By 1940 the division included two armoured brigades, the support group with two motor battalions, an artillery regiment, and an anti-tank regiment. Infantry-support tank battalions and divisional cavalry regiments (light-tank battalions) also fought in northern France. While German success with the Panzer divisions led the British to realize the necessity of expanding their own armoured strength, the British did not understand the importance of combined arms to battlefield success with armour. The limited nature

STUART PITMAN

Born on 16 October 1909, Stuart Alfred Pitman joined the Pitman Press, the family firm, after graduating. After marrying he lived near Tetbury, Gloucestershire. In 1939, he joined the local Territorial Army unit, 2 RGH, in anticipation of a general mobilization. He had no intention of being a soldier and did not go to Sandhurst, but he went with 2 RGH on training and on home-service roles during 1940 and deployed with the regiment to North Africa during the summer of 1941.

Lieutenant Pitman was a member of F Sqn, 2 RGH, during Operation *Crusader*. At the battle of Bir El Gobi (19 November 1941), F Sqn's Major J.W. Saleby, Captain George C.M. Playne and Lieutenant Gerard L. Clay were taken prisoner; Pitman was unwounded. During December, 2 RGH was equipped with US-built M3 Honeys. In late January, the unit was sent to Egypt after Rommel's attack took the Axis forces to the Gazala Line. On 6 February 1942, Pitman was promoted captain. The unit trained on Crusaders, going back to the front in time for the Gazala battles from late May. By 2 June, 2 RGH had lost the Crusaders and had 32 M3 Honeys and 14 M3 Grants. Pitman was in command of B Echelon, the supply unit, though on 4 June he joined the operational squadrons. On 6 June, German 8.8cm guns targeted them, causing many losses; F Sqn's Grants suffered particularly badly.

During July 1942, G Sqn swapped its Honeys for Crusaders and was attached to 9 Lancers; Pitman, along with the other components of 2 RGH, entrained for Egypt. He again commanded B Echelon. On 10 November, after completion of a course he was promoted major and commanded HQ Sqn. Seeing no further combat, 2 RGH was disbanded. Pitman was appointed to Montgomery's staff and deployed to Italy during the summer of 1943.

After 1945 Pitman attended the agricultural college in Cirencester, Gloucestershire, then bought a house and farm near Malmesbury, Wiltshire, because the family home had been destroyed in the war. He was promoted lieutenant-colonel in 1954, commanding 2 RGH. Stuart Pitman died in 1990, aged 81.

of the encounters between German and British armour meant that lessons would not be learnt. Also, some 700 of 1,000 British tanks produced during 1939 and sent to France would be lost; and because of the losses, newly established units had few tanks with which to train.

Although the importance of mounting a 6-pdr rather than a 2-pdr gun was evident before the 1940 campaign, the losses in France meant 2-pdrs had to be continued with because these could be produced in greater quantities. Also, the need was for medium tanks, such as the cruiser, and not heavy tanks mounting larger guns. The German use of armour was beginning to cause a re-appraisal of armour organization, however. After the Dunkirk evacuation (26 May–4 June 1940), armoured brigades added motor battalions to brigade organizations. This did not happen in North Africa, however, because of a lack of infantry.

The other armoured unit Britain had in 1940 was 7th Armoured Division, stationed in Egypt. Pioneers of armoured doctrine stationed in Egypt had some latitude to form and train units the way they wanted. In 1935 when the Italians invaded Ethiopia, the British tank brigade deployed a medium-tank company and light-tank battalion to Egypt and in September 1938 Major-General Hobart was appointed to command the formation, at that point known as the Mobile Division (Egypt). Hobart lacked an infantry battalion and had some problems forcing his training programme on the cavalry regiments. He only stayed for one year, probably because he was not popular, but in that time he did manage to instil into the formation his tactical concepts on the use of armour, especially the principles of mobility and dispersion. These principles could dissipate strength, however, and lead to tank units outpacing other units.

Lessons would not be learnt during the campaign against Italian forces conducted in late 1940 and early 1941. The Italians adopted static positions that gave the British plenty of time to organize set-piece attacks. Only the final engagement was a mobile battle. British and Italian tanks did not fight major tank engagements and did not test armoured doctrine. Neither did 7th Armoured Division fight combined-arms battles.

High morale sustained British operations for eight weeks without stopping. Other armoured units deploying to Egypt would not possess the same unit cohesion or experience of the desert environment as the first iteration of 7th Armoured Division. The formation was brought back to Egypt and 2nd Armoured Division, minus one brigade sent to Greece, arrived in December 1940 and was deployed to Cyrenaica (the eastern part of Libya). The support group was deployed away from the armoured brigade. Hastily organized and having received little or no combined-arms training, this formation did not stand a chance against Generalleutnant Erwin E. Rommel's Panzers and was disbanded on 10 May 1941.

Meanwhile, 7th Armoured Division did not possess any tanks with which to train when withdrawn. Many of its soldiers would be taken as replacements for other units. During 1940 the formation had six regiments; by June 1941 there were four, two of which were new to the division. The two armoured brigades had different missions and different tanks: 4 Armoured Brigade had infantry-support tanks, while 7 Armoured Brigade possessed cruisers and some Crusaders. During Operation *Battleaxe*, 4 Armoured Brigade's mission was to assist the infantry first and then help 7 Armoured Brigade. The different speeds of the tanks made coordination difficult, however.

While both the Germans and British committed the same quantity of tanks with little difference in ability, the Germans had 75 anti-tank guns, the Italians 80 anti-tank guns and the British only 90 2-pdr anti-tank guns. Both British armoured brigades would be defeated by enemy anti-tank gun lines. The destruction of many tanks at long range led British commanders to think that tanks, not anti-tank guns, had hit them; in addition, because enemy tanks were in evidence when British tanks had been targeted at closer ranges, commanders thought enemy tanks had done the damage in these situations. A belief in the superiority of German tanks grew, meaning British commanders thought they needed superior numbers of tanks to beat the enemy. British tankers would be encouraged to close quickly on the enemy to improve their chances of penetrating German tanks; armour units would be separated from supporting infantry and gun batteries. This benefited Italian armour when they operated with the Germans. The British would use tanks to destroy tanks, with armoured brigades manoeuvring alone; the support group would be used to protect lines of communication. The British also needed tanks to guard infantry formations from enemy tanks.

The planning for Operation *Crusader* was dominated by the need to support the infantry. This was to be accomplished by destroying enemy armour before the infantry attack got going. Major-General William H.E. 'Strafer' Gott, GOC 7th Armoured Division, was ordered to do this though the final order took 4 Armoured Brigade – equipped with the US M3 Stuart light tank armed with a 37mm gun and with a range of only 70 miles (113km) – away to protect the infantry. A mission to support the infantry meant 4 Armoured Brigade could not join the armoured battle immediately. The Crusader-equipped 22 Armoured Brigade was newly arrived and only commenced basic desert training on 25 October.

OPPOSITE

These drawings dated 5 November 1942 reveal the Crusader III's turret and fighting compartment. (Tank Museum)

CRUSADER III TURRET

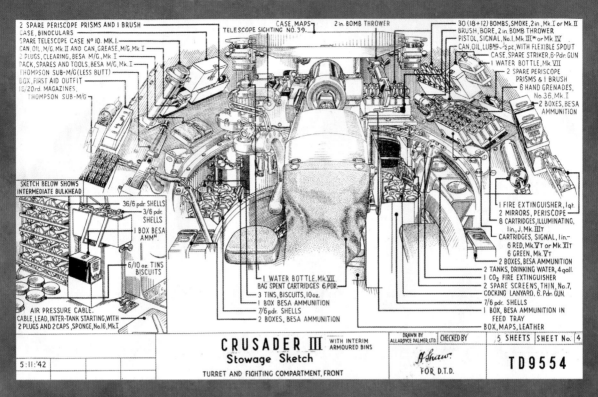

2 SPARE PERISCOPE PRISMS AND I BRUSH
CASE, BINOCULARS
SPARE TELESCOPE CASE Nº 10, MK.I
CAN, OIL, M/G, MK.II AND CAN, GREASE, M/G, MK.I
2 PLUGS, CLEARING, BESA M/G, MK.I
PACK, SPARES AND TOOLS, BESA M/G, MK.I
THOMPSON SUB-M/G (LESS BUTT)
BOX, FIRST AID OUTFIT
16/20rd. MAGAZINES,
THOMPSON SUB-M/G

CASE, MAPS
TELESCOPE SIGHTING NO.39.
2 in. BOMB THROWER

30 (18+12) BOMBS, SMOKE, 2 in., MK.I or MK.II
BRUSH, BORE, 2 in. BOMB THROWER
PISTOL, SIGNAL, No.1, MK.III* or MK.IV
CAN, OIL, LUBNⁿ, ½ pt. WITH FLEXIBLE SPOUT
CASE, SPARE STRIKER, 6-Pdr. GUN
I WATER BOTTLE, MK.VII
2 SPARE PERISCOPE PRISMS & I BRUSH
6 HAND GRENADES, No.36, MK.I
2 BOXES, BESA AMMUNITION

SKETCH BELOW SHOWS INTERMEDIATE BULKHEAD

36/6 pdr. SHELLS
3/6 pdr. SHELLS
I BOX BESA AMMⁿ.
6/10 oz. TINS BISCUITS

I FIRE EXTINGUISHER, 1qt.
2 MIRRORS, PERISCOPE
8 CARTRIDGES, ILLUMINATING, 1 in., J, MK.IIIt
CARTRIDGES, SIGNAL, 1 in.—
6 RED, MK.Vt or MK.XIt
6 GREEN, MK.Vt
2 BOXES, BESA AMMUNITION
2 TANKS, DRINKING WATER, 4gall.
I CO₂ FIRE EXTINGUISHER
2 SPARE SCREENS, THIN, No.7,
COCKING LANYARD, 6, Pdr. GUN.
7/6 pdr. SHELLS
I BOX, BESA AMMUNITION IN FEED TRAY
BOX, MAPS, LEATHER

AIR PRESSURE CABLE.
CABLE, LEAD, INTER-TANK STARTING, WITH
2 PLUGS AND 2 CAPS, SPONGE, No.16, MK.I

I WATER BOTTLE, MK.VII
BAG SPENT CARTRIDGES 6 PDR.
3 TINS, BISCUITS, 10oz.
I BOX BESA AMMUNITION
7/6 pdr. SHELLS
2 BOXES, BESA AMMUNITION

CRUSADER III	WITH INTERIM ARMOURED BINS	DRAWN BY ALLARDYCE PALMER LTD.	CHECKED BY	5 SHEETS	SHEET No. 4
Stowage Sketch		H. Shaw FOR D.T.D.		TD9554	
5:11:'42					
TURRET AND FIGHTING COMPARTMENT, FRONT					

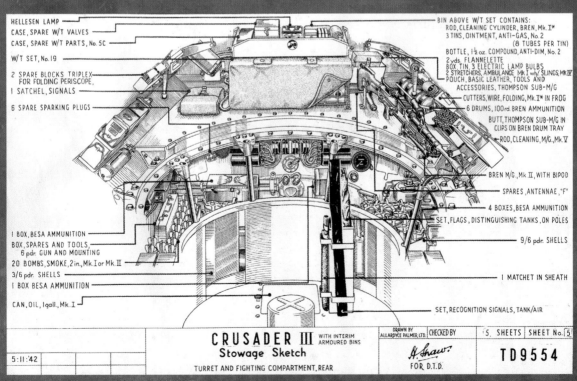

HELLESEN LAMP
CASE, SPARE W/T VALVES
CASE, SPARE W/T PARTS, No. 5C
W/T SET, No.19
2 SPARE BLOCKS TRIPLEX FOR FOLDING PERISCOPE,
I SATCHEL, SIGNALS
6 SPARE SPARKING PLUGS

BIN ABOVE W/T SET CONTAINS:
ROD, CLEANING CYLINDER, BREN, MK.I*
3 TINS, OINTMENT, ANTI-GAS, No.2
(8 TUBES PER TIN)
BOTTLE, 1½ oz. COMPOUND, ANTI-DIM, No.2
2 yds. FLANNELETTE
BOX, TIN, 3 ELECTRIC LAMP BULBS
2 STRETCHERS, AMBULANCE, MK.I w¹/ SLINGS, MK.IV
POUCH, BASIC LEATHER, TOOLS AND ACCESSORIES, THOMPSON SUB-M/G
CUTTERS, WIRE, FOLDING, MK.I* IN FROG
6 DRUMS, 100rd. BREN AMMUNITION
BUTT, THOMPSON SUB-M/G IN CLIPS ON BREN DRUM TRAY
ROD, CLEANING, M/G., MK.V
BREN M/G., MK.II, WITH BIPOD
SPARES, ANTENNAE, "F"
4 BOXES, BESA AMMUNITION
SET, FLAGS, DISTINGUISHING TANKS, ON POLES
9/6 pdr. SHELLS
I MATCHET IN SHEATH
SET, RECOGNITION SIGNALS, TANK/AIR

I BOX, BESA AMMUNITION
BOX, SPARES AND TOOLS, 6pdr. GUN AND MOUNTING
20 BOMBS, SMOKE, 2 in., MK.I or MK.II
3/6 pdr. SHELLS
I BOX BESA AMMUNITION
CAN, OIL, 1gall., MK.I

CRUSADER III	WITH INTERIM ARMOURED BINS	DRAWN BY ALLARDYCE PALMER LTD.	CHECKED BY	5 SHEETS	SHEET No. 5
Stowage Sketch		H. Shaw FOR D.T.D.		TD9554	
5:11:'42					
TURRET AND FIGHTING COMPARTMENT, REAR					

BRITISH TANK TRAINING

Tank crewmen needed to work the tank and fight at the same time. Tanks had to be maintained and technical instruction dominated training schedules. The Training Regiment, Royal Armoured Corps, took new soldiers and had separate wings for maintenance and driving, gunnery, communications and tactics. The last of these was the domain of the tank commander; the crew often obeyed his orders with little awareness of the tactical situation. Only when trainees got to the field units did they begin to appreciate other roles and understand the way in which they fitted into the smooth operation of the unit.

Instruction at the Armoured Fighting Vehicle Gunnery School in Lulworth Camp, Dorset, concentrated on firing while in motion. Training at battle ranges involved practising fighting against other tanks, though this occurred for only two weeks a year. More time was spent at local ranges, though mostly these used only static targets. After the battle of Gazala, Major-General McCreery criticized shoulder-controlled gunnery as most firing was done while stationary (Knight 2015: 72).

Linney Head in Pembrokeshire was the best-known battle range. Tank commanders sought to appreciate the ground, use maps, direct other tanks by using the radio and operate the tank effectively. When a tank was in motion, performing these tasks was difficult. Limited training time was partly because the War Office set limits on track mileage to limit wear. Also, the supply of ammunition was restricted to limit wear on gun barrels. Land suitable for conducting training was not abundant; if a unit was not close to a training area, then this hampered the maintenance of a useful training schedule. From 1941, other training grounds were established, helping to ameliorate the situation. The number of battle ranges also expanded, in line with the number of armoured units.

Mocked-up targets were fired at by multiple tanks, limiting the ability to detect poor performance by some. Also, the unit's commanding officer would judge the use of ground; keeping an eye on so many tanks could lead him to focus on the better commanders, not the least effective. GHQ instructions stated that only eight umpires were needed for a unit of 52 tanks. This meant that minor tactics could not be tested effectively. Minor tactics would be used profusely on the battlefield by tank commanders as doctrine stated that armour would operate without much support by other arms. Only when Lieutenant-General Bernard L. Montgomery took charge in North Africa did he attempt to end this approach, though different training priorities continued to be pursued by cruiser brigades and infantry-support brigades. For cruiser brigades, exploitation and pursuit were the guiding principles.

Formed on 3 September 1939, 22 Armoured Brigade included three Territorial Army units: 2 RGH operated alongside 3rd and 4th County of London Yeomanry (3 and 4 CLY). The equipment and training of 22 Armoured Brigade proceeded slowly because with most armour lost in France during 1940, units needed to be on invasion watch. The brigade got its first cruiser tanks, Mk IVAs, at the end of 1940. By the spring of 1941 the brigade was located in Wiltshire. By 1 June, 3 CLY had 16 Crusaders, 26 light tanks, ten scout cars and seven personnel carriers, along with 65 lorries and 17 motorcycles. In mid-August the brigade embarked for North Africa

British tankers enjoy a break near a Crusader I/II sporting a camouflage paint scheme. The small size of the 2-pdr gun is evident. (The Tank Museum 5938 A4)

having received many Crusaders late, just before embarkation, straight from the assembly lines. Each regiment had a headquarters squadron with four Crusaders and two close-support Crusaders, and three squadrons each with a squadron headquarters with two Crusaders and two close-support Crusaders, and three platoons each with four Crusaders.

Lieutenant-Colonel Charles Birley's 2 RGH arrived in Egypt on 1 October 1941. Only a single crane was capable of unloading the Crusaders at dockside. This took two weeks and the crews went ahead to camp. After three weeks the tanks turned up. The majority needed oil filters, track-guard inserts, gear-lever extensions and fan assemblies to be fitted by base workshops. The crews drove the Crusaders 40km to a training site to conduct brigade training and gunnery. This consisted of seizing a piece of ground and forcing the 'enemy' to attack them. Little time was spent training before Operation *Crusader* commenced.

BRITISH ORGANIZATION

The combined-arms units the Italians and Germans deployed during Operation *Crusader* depleted Eighth Army's tank brigades, though General der Panzertruppe Rommel made an operational mistake by driving for the Egyptian border. He had to withdraw because of the threat to his lines of communication. The British recovered, albeit having lost some 800 tanks, and Rommel was on his way west and out of Cyrenaica. After Operation *Crusader*, 7th Armoured Division was again withdrawn to Egypt. A new formation, 2 Armoured Brigade, was ordered to Cyrenaica. Elements of 22 Armoured Brigade also helped with its defence, but no British support group was sent to Cyrenaica. Rommel again trounced the British armour, causing the loss of 70 tanks and gaining moral ascendancy. Many wondered if the tactical leadership of

This close-support Crusader has a two-tone camouflage paint scheme that also extends to its wheels. Note the hull-mounted Besa machine-gun auxiliary turret. Smoke was a necessity and could be used by Crusader close-support variants. Range for smoke was up to 1,600yd (1,463m), while range for high-explosive ammunition was up to 2,400yd (2,195m). By the summer of 1942, the Crusader squadron usually operated two close-support Crusaders with the squadron headquarters. Grant headquarters platoons could also be composed of two 2-pdr Crusaders and two close-support Crusaders. (The Tank Museum 4379-E3)

British armoured units could compete with the Germans, though the Italians were not viewed in the same light. Once again, British tank units were dismantled to be sent to other units as replacements, thus dissipating unit cohesion gained during training.

During the May–June 1942 Gazala operation, armoured units officially included a single armoured brigade and a motorized-infantry brigade. The armoured brigade had its own motorized-infantry battalion. The brigades also had artillery regiments assigned. This organization meant brigades could fight alone, though combat support assets would be dispersed and could not be massed. The 6-pdr anti-tank gun was not yet operational, meaning 25-pdr batteries had to be used in the anti-tank gun role to destroy enemy tanks. This was not the 25-pdr's proper purpose.

By August 1942, Grant tanks equipped A Sqn and B Sqn and Crusaders C Sqn of most tank regiments. Crusaders would lead the way, accompanied by a forward observation tank for the artillery. Royal Engineer detachments would follow with the reserve platoon of Crusader tanks. The regimental headquarters would be next, with three columns slightly further back. On the left was an infantry company in lorries, the middle column was an artillery battery from the Royal Horse Artillery and the right column was an anti-tank battery. A Sqn on the right and B Sqn on the left protected the three columns. By October 1942, the Sherman was issued to most units, usually equipping one squadron alongside a Grant squadron and a Crusader squadron. Some Crusaders armed with the 6-pdr gun would also be deployed, fighting as part of the Crusader squadron.

For the Second Battle of El Alamein (23 October–11 November 1942), Montgomery fielded the bulk of his armour in a single formation incorporating 1st, 8th and 10th Armoured divisions. His doctrine, instilled by enforcing a rigorous training regime, specified that commanders would make rapid decisions, issuing orders based on an appreciation of the changing situation. The Eighth Army's infantry needed to clear the minefields so British armour could get at the enemy gun line. Infantry with the support of 6-pdr anti-tank guns would also be used to seize ground to entice Axis armour to attack.

ITALIAN ARMOUR DOCTRINE

During the 1920s, Italian military writers thought tanks would support the infantry. Colonnello Enrico Maltese, head of the Reparto Carri Armati (Tank Department), believed that tanks would be used in a scouting role, to be deployed with the infantry and not as separate entities. Only when Mussolini demanded a military capable of conquering new territory did the theory of a large mobile armoured unit capable of winning quick victories gain prominence. Colonnello Sebastino Visconti Prasca published articles in 1934 calling for the armour to break the enemy line and create a gap for other forces. Drawing upon experience gained during the Second Italo-Ethiopian War (1935–37), the new doctrine was further articulated during 1938–39. On 28 October 1938, high-speed mobile warfare became the official strategic and tactical concept of the Italian Army.

Generale di divisione Rudolf Graziani, who during the invasion of Ethiopia was commander of the Southern Front defending Somalia, was not happy with a static role; but with 60,000 men to defend an 800km frontier, he was not expected to go on the attack. This was the aim of the Northern Front group of forces, nearly double the size of Graziani's command. On his own initiative, he bought lorries and formed motorized columns to travel through the Ogaden Desert. During April 1936 Graziani's troops employed combined-arms teams followed by infantry to assault Ethiopian positions from forward bases located within the desert. Generale di brigata Guglielmo Nasi used the motorized columns to encircle attacking Ethiopian forces while Italian infantry met them head-on. The Ethiopian army defending the south was defeated. L3 tankettes supported the Italian motorized infantry though they could not lead the assault.

The Second Italo-Ethiopian War lasted a long time and to win a European war the leadership needed to develop a highly mobile force like the Italian expeditionary force sent to assist the Nationalists during the Spanish Civil War (1936–39). Mobile forces had some successes in Spain; on 7 February 1937 they exploited through a sparsely defended enemy line when a battalion of L3s took Malaga with infantry support. In April 1937, 60 Italian tanks were used on the road to Madrid though they were defeated by Soviet tanks equipped with proper guns and not just machine guns. These operations showed the importance of using armour to lead the assault. An Italian doctrine comparable to the German armoured doctrine was being articulated. Rapid assault forces would hit weak points of

Italian tankers are pictured with their tankettes and signalling flags. (The Tank Museum 3186 D6)

PIETRO BRUNO

Born in 1920, Pietro Bruno was brought up in Aidone, Sicily. He studied law at the University of Catania, though he abandoned his studies in the fourth year to join the Italian Army in August 1940. He attended an officer cadet course with the 3° Reggimento fanteria carristo at Bologna. This unit had the task of training officer students and NCOs. He graduated with the rank of *sottotenente* in March 1941.

In July 1941, Bruno was sent to North Africa to fight with the 'Ariete' Armoured Division. Taking command of a platoon of L3/35 tankettes, he was near Bir el Gobi, though his unit was not deployed against Crusaders during the battle. He was awarded the *Croce di guerra al valor militare* for demonstrating heroic military conduct directly after battle. After his unit was disbanded on 8 January 1942, he went to the tank school and from April 1942 the Centro di Istruzione Carristi (Tank Instruction Centre). Some 70 Italian officers had joined this training facility at Corradini at the Homs Oasis, tasked with training personnel and supplying tanks to the Italian Army units operating in North Africa.

Bruno then joined the X Battaglione carristi during the summer of 1942. He commanded a platoon of 1ª Compagnia, equipped with M14/41s. He won the *Medaglia d'argento al valor militare* for taking personal risks, leaning out of the turret to better direct his tanks, on 4 November 1942, during the Second Battle of El Alamein. He was wounded in the head by shrapnel, but continued to command his tank, directing the gunner onto targets. Bruno was being treated for his injuries when his tank was hit by an enemy armour-piercing shot, penetrating the tank and fatally wounding him.

The *Medaglia d'oro al valor militare alla memoria* was awarded to Bruno for skilful and reckless manoeuvres at the same battle. He had accompanied a section of Semovente 75/18 self-propelled guns onto the Allied flank in order for the battalion to disengage from a numerically superior enemy. In 1975, X Battaglione carri M.O. Bruno was established, named after him.

OPPOSITE

These photographs reveal details of the M14/40's interior: (**1**) position of Marelli RF 1 CA radio set; (**2**) machine-gun ammunition storage; (**3**) turret rotation wheel; (**4**) attachment for 47/32 gun elevating gear; (**5**) 47/32 gun; (**6**) turret hatch; (**7**) sliding doors for 47/32 gun ammunition; (**8**) armoured vision slot (closed); (**9**) driver's seat; (**10**) machine-gunner's seat; (**11**) commander's seat (missing); (**12**) loader's seat. (Tank Museum 6284-A6 & 6284-B2)

the enemy line and combined arms would neutralize enemy efforts to stop them through concentrated and coordinated fires. Armoured divisions supported by motorized divisions would be used to assault the enemy line. *Celere* (rapid) divisions, composed of cavalry, motorized light infantry, armoured cars and motorized artillery, would be used in the exploitation role.

By 1940, the *divisione corazzata* (armoured division) was a balanced formation combining tanks, motorized infantry and artillery, with supporting units such as engineers, who trained and operated together. According to doctrine, armoured formations had to be combined-arms formations, with a balance of tanks, guns and infantry, training and operating in concert with each other. The Italian armoured division included a tank regiment with three battalions, making a total of 157 tanks; an artillery regiment of three groups; a *Bersaglieri* motorized light-infantry regiment of three battalions; engineer, anti-tank and transport battalions; and medical and supply units. The first armoured division to be established, on 1 February 1939, was the 132ª Divisione corazzata 'Ariete'. The other two armoured divisions, 131ª 'Centauro' and 133ª 'Littorio', were also formed during 1939. During the 1939 exercises, the armour and supporting motorized infantry attacked south of the Po River into the Apennines, through terrain over which they thought the next war would be fought. The L5/21s and L3s used were acknowledged to be obsolete, however. The problem was the lack of a medium tank. The M13/40 was the solution.

While no Italian armoured or motorized divisions were sent to Libya in 1940, 322 L3s and 17 armoured cars had deployed by June, primarily operating in independent tank battalions assigned to the infantry divisions. Generale di brigata Pietro Maletti's

M14/41 TURRET

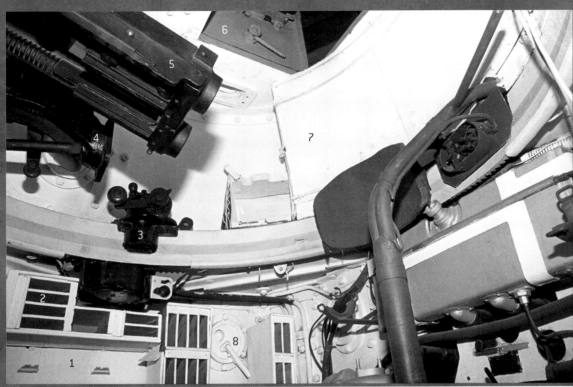

motorized *Raggruppamento* (grouping), composed of one tank battalion and seven motorized-infantry battalions, was an exception. By 13 September 1940, when the Italians invaded Egypt, four light-tank battalions were still assigned to the infantry, with three others along with three motorized-infantry battalions and two medium-tank battalions making up the *Comando Carri Armati della Libia* (Libyan Tank Command). This was composed of 1° Raggruppamento Carristi with two battalions, one with light tanks and the other with medium tanks; 2° Raggruppamento Carristi, with two battalions of light tanks; and Maletti's *Raggruppamento* with one medium-tank battalion and three motorized-infantry battalions. On 18 November, the Raggruppamento Babini would also be formed with two tank battalions of M13/40s, two light-tank battalions, two gun groups and three battalions of mobile infantry.

Graziani's staff explored the possibilities of using tanks and motorized infantry rather than non-motorized infantry to form a mobile column to conduct the attack into Egypt. His staff estimated they had enough lorries to form two motorized-infantry divisions. Graziani turned down this option, though a plan to use Raggruppamento Maletti on a sweep through the desert to turn the British defences was approved. This effort failed when the proper maps did not get distributed and the Italian force got lost. Though it did not comply with the doctrine, Graziani sent his infantry *en masse* along the coast road on 13 September. Partially motorized infantry led the way, using shuttle runs to make progress. 1° Raggruppamento Carristi was out in front with Raggruppamento Maletti at the rear. Graziani decided to build fortified camps at Sidi Barrani and wait for the British counter-attack, thereby passing up the opportunity to form mobile groups according to doctrine to push further on when the British armour was not up to strength. Instead, the British were able to deploy Matilda II infantry tanks no Italian anti-tank gun could knock out. Italian military intelligence had exaggerated the British strength, however, basing it on the number of convoys sent to Egypt and not on the equipment disembarked. Graziani was encouraged to think he needed mass to deal with his enemy.

ITALIAN TANK TRAINING

The M13/40 crews received basic training. From 1939, a series of tank training courses was prepared at Bracciano, north-west of Rome. Only a single M13/40 was available, so during their training, tank commanders fired only five rounds from the 47mm gun and one magazine from the 8mm machine gun. Drivers, gunners and machine-gunners each fired three 47mm rounds and one machine-gun magazine. Two courses, each lasting one month, were held between December 1939 and February 1940. When Italy joined the war in June 1940, the courses were laid on again, from 15 July, each lasting 19 days. The courses were held at the Ansaldo factory in Genoa, again using a single M13/40, though some others were borrowed from the production line. Three courses were held prior to the resumption of the course at Bracciano. A course for mechanics, with ten days spent at the tank training centre, seven at the Ansaldo Factory in Genoa and seven at the SPA engine plant in Turin, was also established. By late 1940, drivers and mechanics took courses at Bologna. During

A *tenente* from the 'Ariete' Armoured Division poses with his tankers. (Colaimages/Alamy Stock Photo)

1941, other organizations provided lessons for tank drivers, including the Motorization Studies Centre in Rome, and the Tank Training Centre in Civitavecchia. When personnel were assigned to units, three gunnery lessons were supposed to be organized. By early 1942, training centres in North Africa were established to tailor instruction to operational conditions – especially useful in the training of crews transitioning from the L3 tankette to the M13/40.

Combined-arms training was almost non-existent for the early ad hoc motorized formations such as Raggruppamento Babini. The early combined-arms columns would suffer because no standard battle drills existed. While Italian doctrine stipulated the cooperation of medium tanks with artillery and infantry, no training brought these elements together. Only when armour from the 'Ariete' Armoured Division was sent to Libya did groups with proper combined-arms training appear. Training was inconsistent, however, with enforcement of a common standard lacking. Command and control was not developed and the means of communication needed to support these operations was limited.

Tank formations trained to attack in company formations, each company deploying on a frontage of 400m or two companies over 1,000m. The other companies would be used to follow on. When on the march, either a column or line could be adopted depending on the uncertainty of the situation. The companies could also deploy echeloned to the right or left. With experience, a line with both flanks slightly back would be adopted. By the summer of 1941, the tank battalion was 52 tanks strong, with four in battalion headquarters, and 16 in each of three companies. Each company had a command tank and three platoons each with five tanks. The regimental headquarters had three tanks and commanded three battalions, with another 33 tanks supposed to be in reserve. This made for a theoretical strength of 192 tanks. In reality, the 'Ariete' Armoured Division had only 141 medium tanks within its 132° Reggimento fanteria carrista when Operation *Crusader* commenced. Medium tanks simply did not exist in the numbers needed.

ITALIAN ORGANIZATION

By September 1941, Axis forces in North Africa consisted of Rommel's Deutsches Afrikakorps and the Italian Corpo d'Armata di Manovra (Manoeuvre Army Corps) and XXI Corpo d'armata; X Corpo d'armata was added during 1941. The Deutsches Afrikakorps would number 54,000 men at most, during mid-1942. In late 1941 it consisted of 15. and 21. Panzer-Divisionen and 90. leichte Division; 164. leichte Division would also be deployed by September 1942. Established on 10 September 1941 and subordinate to Generale di armata Ettore Bastico, commander of the Comando Superiore Africa Settentrionale, the Corpo d'Armata di Manovra was commanded by Generale di divisione Gastone Gambara, who was also Bastico's chief of staff. Gambara's command included the 'Ariete' Armoured Division, later joined by the 'Littorio' Armoured Division and the 'Trieste' Motorized Division. The 'Ariete' Armoured Division would fight on until it was destroyed on 4 November 1942, buying time for the German units to escape from El Alamein. The 'Littorio' Armoured Division experienced the same fate.

At first, the 'Ariete' Armoured Division had L3/35 tankettes armed only with machine guns. Deployed to North Africa from January–February 1941, the division fought for the first time on 7 April. The division then attacked Tobruk unsuccessfully and besieged the city's port. From late July 1941, the division was commanded by Generale di brigata Mario Balotta. In September 1941, the division organized a further tank regiment equipped with M13/40 medium tanks. Tenente colonnello Enrico Maretti commanded the 132° Reggimento fanteria carrista, with 146 M13/40s. The light-tank regiment was gradually phased out. The 'Ariete' Armoured Division could also deploy 16 105/28 Mod. 1913 guns, 32 75/27 Mod. 1911 guns and eight 47/32 Mod. 1935 guns.

The 'Littorio' Armoured Division arrived in North Africa in early 1942, but had to let its X Battaglione carri, the *Bersaglieri* support-weapons battalion, two self-propelled-gun groups and the single lorry-mounted 90/53 gun group go to the 'Ariete' Armoured Division. 'Ariete' disbanded the VII Battaglione carri because of losses. During late 1941, the tanks of 'Littorio's XII Battaglione carri were lost en route to North Africa when the ship carrying them was torpedoed and sank. 'Littorio' was allocated the IV and LI Battaglioni carri from the 'Centauro' Armoured Division; the LI Battaglione carri would be operational by May and the IV Battaglione carri by August. By May 1942, the XII Battaglione carri was also re-formed. The 'Ariete' Armoured Division's VIII Battaglione carri was disbanded in July 1942 and the XIII Battaglione carri from the 'Centauro' Armoured Division was sent out to take its place, though not in time for the Second Battle of El Alamein.

Generale di brigata Mario Balotta, the commander of the 'Ariete' Armoured Division from July 1941 until January 1942, is pictured with one of the tanks under his command. (Amb2012/Wikimedia/ CC BY-SA 4.0)

THE STRATEGIC SITUATION

On 13 September 1940, Italian forces advanced from Libya along the coast road. They had 150,000 men against the 36,000-strong British Western Desert Force. The Italians soon halted at Sidi Barrani and proceeded to build a road. The British armoured force of 248 light tanks and medium cruiser tanks worried the Italian command. Most believed that armour would be the battle winner on the desert plains; with few natural features to defend, the infantry would be exposed and potentially overrun by enemy armour. The Italian command urgently asked for medium tanks to be sent to counter the British cruisers. Four battalions' worth of M13/40s were disembarked, though some did not get to the front prior to the British counter-attack on 6 December 1940. Meanwhile, the highly mobile 7th Armoured Division ran rings around the static Italian positions. On 19 January 1941, Mussolini asked Germany for military help. Three days later, Allied forces seized Tobruk and took 25,000 Italian personnel prisoner. Between 2 and 8 February, ships with equipment belonging to the 'Ariete' Armoured Division reached Tripoli harbour. Initially armed with L3 tankettes, the division received a battalion of M13/40s by mid-March. As the Italians attempted to withdraw from Cyrenaica, the British stopped them at Beda Fomm on 6 February and the Italian army was destroyed.

Only a motley group of Italian stragglers halted at Sirte. Rommel disembarked in Tripoli on 12 February and would command the 5. leichte Division and 15. Panzer-Division, due to disembark fully by the spring. On 16 February, the first German elements reached Sirte. The British meanwhile had sent units to Greece and Ethiopia. On 24 March Rommel seized El Agheila; he then formed mobile columns to stop the

British from withdrawing from Benghazi by motoring through the desert to the Egyptian frontier.

The Italians formed mixed columns of lorry-borne infantry and guns. While light tanks operated with them, the medium tanks would suffer abnormally high rates of mechanical failure because the crews were unfamiliar with desert operating conditions. For example, the VII Battaglione carri, while attached to Panzer-Regiment 5, had only seven working M13/40s out of 50 by the time the battalion reached the Tobruk area because the Italians did not possess proper oil filters and the crews had no experience of the desert.

In mid-April, elements of the 'Ariete' Armoured Division, supported by infantry from the 102ᵃ Divisione motorizzata 'Trento', attacked the Tobruk perimeter fortifications. These attacks continued until mid-May, though the Australian defenders often mounted counter-attacks, seeking to isolate the Italian armour from the infantry. The Tobruk defences held, though British attempts to use armour to lift the siege during June failed primarily because of the presence of a strong German and Italian gun line. Rommel used the next four months to plan a full-scale attack on Tobruk. He did not know that the British were also planning an offensive.

The 'Ariete' Armoured Division used this time to form 132° Reggimento fanteria carrista, equipped with 141 M13/40s. The VII Battaglione carri was joined by the VIII Battaglione carri during June and by the IX Battaglione carri in October. They would defeat 22 Armoured Brigade at Bir el Gobi on 19 November, soon after Operation *Crusader* commenced; because it lacked sufficient infantry and gun support, the British armoured brigade was badly depleted during the battle. The Allied plan to lift the siege of Tobruk was derailed, though constant attacks by Allied infantry formations wore down the German and Italian forces nearer the coast. The siege was lifted by 10 December and Rommel withdrew first to Gazala and then to Agedabia by 27 December. By this stage, the 'Ariete' Armoured Division had only one platoon's worth of tanks functioning, with others in need of repair; the Germans had 70 tanks operational. By 1 January 1942, the Axis forces had withdrawn to El Agheila.

In late 1941, the 'Littorio' Armoured Division was sent to Tripoli with 90 M14/41s disembarking along with two groups of Semovente 75/18 self-propelled guns. On 14 December 1941 the division's XII Battaglione carri was lost when the British submarine HMS *Upright* sank the Italian merchantman *Fabio Filzi* with 52 M14/41s on board. The 'Littorio' Armoured Division was not deployed to the front; instead, most of its tanks were sent to the 'Ariete' Armoured Division. With these new forces, Rommel counter-attacked on 19 January 1942. British formations, further from base, had not enough time to replenish and inexperienced units held the line. By 29 January the 'Ariete' Armoured Division occupied Benghazi. On 4 February, the British withdrew to the Gazala Line, having lost 77 tanks and 192 guns during Rommel's counter-attack.

The Gazala Line consisted of brigade boxes with armour deployed between them. The Germans had 409 tanks and the Italians 189 M13/40s or M14/41s and 39 L6 light tanks, excluding those elements of the 'Littorio' Armoured Division not yet deployed to the front line. The British had 167 Grants, 149 Stuarts and 257 Crusaders as part of 1st and 7th Armoured divisions. They also had 276 infantry-support tanks serving with 1 Tank Brigade and 32 Tank Brigade. The British total (including reserve

A Crusader I/II with supply vehicles. Two sets of stowage bins on the mudguards and fuel drums on the back identify this as a late-production tank. (The Tank Museum 5938-A6)

models) was 994 tanks with another 300 expected, yet Generaloberst Rommel swept around the British line with his German and Italian armoured forces on 27 May.

The 'Ariete' Armoured Division, alongside German motorized and tank formations, occupied the area later termed the 'Cauldron', located among the British defences. Within this area was the 150 Infantry Brigade box, which was attacked primarily by the German units while the 'Ariete' Armoured Division guarded Aslagh Ridge, establishing a gun line facing eastwards with armour held on the other side of the ridge to hold off British counter-attacks. The deployment worked when on 30 May, the British attacked the ridge, losing 57 tanks in the process. The 150 Infantry Brigade box collapsed on 1 June, though attempts to destroy Rommel in the Cauldron continued until 12 June. The British armour was gradually worn down. On 12 June the German Panzers broke the British line and Tobruk was isolated by 19 June. The 'Littorio' Armoured Division, with the XII and LI Battaglioni carri, two *Bersaglieri* battalions and the weak 133° Reggimento artiglieria, was committed to the perimeter around Tobruk. The Allied garrison decided to surrender on 22 June. A port capable of accepting supplies close to the front line would soon be at Rommel's disposal.

By 25 June, because of constant combat attrition, the Italians had only one battalion's worth of M14/41s operational and German armour was in a similar state. Yet Generalfeldmarschall Rommel pursued the British to Mersa Matruh, capturing the Egyptian town on 29 June. On 30 June, 4 Armoured Brigade attacked the 'Littorio' Armoured Division; the LI Battaglione carri suffered losses and 'Littorio' had only ten M14/41s operational. On 26 May, the Italians had 240 operational tanks, and by 1 July only 80. German tank strength was 295 on 26 May and just 37 on 1 July. By 1 July, the British had only 137 tanks with units, 42 going to units from base workshops and 902 sitting in base workshops. With these tanks back up and running, the British would deploy a potentially crushing superiority.

Egypt was now exposed, with the Suez Canal in Rommel's sights. The British were able to establish a proper defence line between the Qattara Depression and the Mediterranean to stop him. Rommel's attack on 1 July was held. Rommel's infantry, supported by his Panzers, held the line against British assaults throughout the rest of July.

By late August 1942, Rommel had 510 tanks (281 Italian, including 38 light tanks, and 229 German, including 29 light tanks); Eighth Army had 1,038 tanks, including 170 M3 Grants and 252 M4 Shermans. Not to be deterred, Rommel launched most of his armour at British positions astride Alam el Halfa Ridge. The Axis attack was a costly failure. Many British tanks could be brought back to operational status by the workshops, however. Through to October, both sides replenished their losses and by the middle of that month the Italians had 278 M13/40s and M14/41s, the Germans 249 tanks and the British 1,029. When the Second Battle of El Alamein commenced on 23 October, the 'Littorio' Armoured Division was stationed to the north in the second echelon; the LI Battaglione carri was equipped with M13/40s, and the IV and XII Battaglioni carri with M14/41s. Two groups, each with nine Semovente 75/18 self-propelled guns, supported them. The Italian artillery fielded 12 75/27 Mod. 1911, eight 100/17 Mod. 14 and ten German 88/55 guns. Italian infantry forces consisted of three *Bersaglieri* battalions. The 'Littorio' Armoured Division was supported by 15. Panzer-Division. The 'Ariete' Armoured Division was deployed to the south, between El Mireir and Qarat el Himeimat, with 21. Panzer-Division nearby.

Lieutenant-General Montgomery's planning for the Second Battle of El Alamein involved the Allied infantry first assaulting Miteiriya Ridge manned by Axis infantry battalions. By 25 October, the 'Littorio' Armoured Division was committed against breaches made in the line by 2 Armoured Brigade supported by 7 Motor Brigade and 9th Australian Division elements. The IV Battaglione carri faced 10th Armoured Division, committed to destroy the Axis gun line. The XII Battaglione carri, supported by self-propelled guns, fought at Kidney Ridge. On 27 October, the German and Italian armour counter-attacked strongly held Allied positions. The British used artillery barrages and flew air sorties to interdict the Italian deployments. Meanwhile the 'Ariete' Armoured Division began to shift northwards to assist the 'Littorio' Armoured Division. On 2 November, Montgomery launched Operation *Supercharge*, with 578 tanks on the front line against 90 German and 189 Italian tanks. At Tell el Aqqaqir, 35 German and 65 Italian tanks met the British 9 Armoured Brigade, equipped with 130 Sherman, Grant and Crusader tanks. By the end of the day, 'Littorio' had just one company's worth of tanks operational.

Having not been substantially involved in the battle to this point, the 'Ariete' Armoured Division was ordered to assemble at Deir el Murra to guard the withdrawal of Axis infantry to Fuka. On 4 November, 'Ariete' was attacked by 4 Light Armoured Brigade supported by 22 Armoured Brigade. The Italians could not maintain a line and were enveloped. The M14/41s could not stand up to the superior British tanks, including the Crusader III. At 1530hrs, a radio message from the Italians signified the end, out of ammunition and surrounded near Bir el Abd; the battle was lost, though some Axis tanks disengaged successfully. The Germans managed to withdraw, partly because the 'Ariete' Armoured Division had stood firm. On 5 November, surviving Italian armoured elements fought 8 Armoured Brigade and suffered further losses. On 21 November, both the 'Ariete' and 'Littorio' Armoured divisions were disbanded. Rommel's withdrawal saw his units flee from Egypt to Tunisia. Mussolini had decided to deploy the battalions of the 'Centauro' Armoured Division not yet sent, though the formation only disembarked after the battle was over.

Intended as a supplement to the Italian Army's medium tanks, the Semovente 75/18 was inspired by the German Sturmgeschütz III. (Photo 12/Universal Images Group via Getty Images)

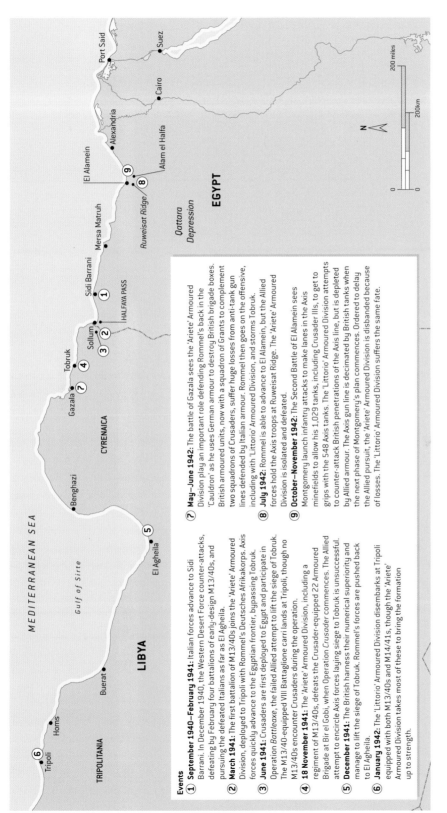

MEDITERRANEAN SEA

Gulf of Sirte

LIBYA

TRIPOLITANIA

CYRENAICA

Homs • Tripoli • Buerat

Benghazi •

El Agheila ⑤

Gazala ⑦ • Tobruk ④
Sollum ③ ② • Sidi Barrani ①
HALFAYA PASS

EGYPT

Mersa Matruh •

Ruweisat Ridge ⑧ ⑨ • El Alamein
Alam el Halfa •

Qattara Depression

Alexandria • Port Said •
Cairo • Suez •

N

0 — 200 miles
0 — 200km

Events

① **September 1940–February 1941:** Italian forces advance to Sidi Barrani. In December 1940, the Western Desert Force counter-attacks, defeating by February four battalions of early-design M13/40s, and pursuing the defeated Italians as far as El Agheila.

② **March 1941:** The first battalion of M13/40s joins the 'Ariete' Armoured Division, deployed to Tripoli with Rommel's Deutsches Afrikakorps. Axis forces quickly advance to the Egyptian frontier, bypassing Tobruk.

③ **June 1941:** Crusaders are first deployed to Egypt and participate in Operation *Battleaxe*, the failed Allied attempt to lift the siege of Tobruk. The M13/40-equipped VIII Battaglione carri lands at Tripoli, though no M13/40s encounter Crusaders during the operation.

④ **18 November 1941:** The 'Ariete' Armoured Division, including a regiment of M13/40s, defeats the Crusader-equipped 22 Armoured Brigade at Bir el Gobi, when Operation *Crusader* commences. The Allied attempt to encircle Axis forces laying siege to Tobruk is unsuccessful.

⑤ **December 1941:** The British harness their numerical superiority and manage to lift the siege of Tobruk. Rommel's forces are pushed back to El Agheila.

⑥ **January 1942:** The 'Littorio' Armoured Division disembarks at Tripoli equipped with both M13/40s and M14/41s, though the 'Ariete' Armoured Division takes most of these to bring the formation up to strength.

⑦ **May–June 1942:** The battle of Gazala sees the 'Ariete' Armoured Division play an important role defending Rommel's back in the 'Cauldron' as he uses German armour to destroy British brigade boxes. British armoured units, now with a squadron of Grants to complement two squadrons of Crusaders, suffer huge losses from anti-tank gun lines defended by Italian armour. Rommel then goes on the offensive, including with 'Littorio' Armoured Division, and storms Tobruk.

⑧ **July 1942:** Rommel is able to advance to El Alamein, but the Allied forces hold the Axis troops at Ruweisat Ridge. The 'Ariete' Armoured Division is isolated and defeated.

⑨ **October–November 1942:** The Second Battle of El Alamein sees Montgomery launch infantry attacks to make lanes in the Axis minefields to allow his 1,029 tanks, including Crusader IIIs, to get to grips with the 548 Axis tanks. The 'Littorio' Armoured Division attempts to counter-attack British penetrations of the Axis line, but is depleted by Allied armour. The Axis gun line is decimated by British tanks when the next phase of Montgomery's plan commences. Ordered to delay the Allied pursuit, the 'Ariete' Armoured Division is disbanded because of losses. The 'Littorio' Armoured Division suffers the same fate.

This map shows the course of the North Africa campaign in 1941–42.

COMBAT

OPERATION *CRUSADER*

Operation *Crusader* was intended to lift the siege of Tobruk. Ordered to swing around the right (west) of the Axis defences and occupy Gabr Saleh, 7th Armoured Division was to take ground astride the Axis supply lines and thereby force Axis tank formations to mount a counter-attack. The 770 tanks fielded by the British faced 418 Axis tanks (272 German, including about 70 light tanks, plus 146 Italian medium tanks; the 162 Italian L3/35s could not face Allied armour). Rommel was also planning a new attack on Tobruk and had gathered German armour near the port. He had asked the 'Ariete' Armoured Division to defend the frontier against possible attack by British infantry approaching the road intersection at Bir el Gobi. Occupying the southernmost point of the Axis line alongside Italian infantry formations, 'Ariete' began to entrench during early November 1941.

Based on signals intercepts and other sources, the Italian intelligence detachment headed by Maggiore Mario Revetria suggested that the British would soon launch an offensive with armour. Rommel did not accept this and went on leave during late October. He was determined to commence his attack on Tobruk, despite protests from the Italians. Rommel got back just before the British launched the operation. Intelligence suggested to him that there was nothing to worry about. On 17 November, a storm turned the ground to mud and strong winds made flying impossible, which meant Axis aerial reconnaissance could not confirm the gathering of British forces on the frontier.

Generale di divisione Gambara, commander of the Corpo d'Armata di Manovra, placed his men on high alert. On the morning of 18 November, Rommel ordered the

'Ariete' Armoured Division to displace to the south-east of Bir el Gobi. Gambara did not obey the order – at the time he did not answer to Rommel, instead taking orders from the Comando Superiore Africa Settentrionale – as he thought the intelligence assessment of a British attack by his intelligence department was correct. Eight days previously, 'Ariete' had deployed to Bir el Gobi, where the Trigh el Abd and the Tobruk–Giarabub roads met. The Italian armoured division had dug emplacements and determined lines of sight, taking note of slight undulations in the ground, to the east of Bir el Gobi. They also had a 75/27 Mod. 1911 gun group from the 'Pavia' Infantry Division, a 105/28 Mod. 1913 gun group from army-level command and a battery of lorry-mounted 102/35 Mod. 1914 guns manned by naval militia personnel. Gambara deployed the 132° Reggimento fanteria carrista about 10km north-west of Bir el Gobi.

An Italian Mod. 1935 tankers' helmet with leather skirting, a padded brow bumper and tall leather bowl. The bumper was known to offer good protection and the design was sturdy, with the bumper stitched firmly to the helmet. (INTERFOTO/Alamy Stock Photo)

The Italians had three battalion strongpoints to the east, south-east and south-west of Bir el Gobi. In the south-east was the V Battaglione of the 8° Reggimento bersaglieri with a company of 47/32 Mod. 1935 anti-tank guns and the II Gruppo of the 132° Reggimento artiglieria with 75/27 Mod. 1911 guns. To the east was the III Battaglione armi d'accompagnamento with a company of 47/32 Mod. 1935 anti-tank guns and the 75/27 Mod. 1911 gun group from the 'Pavia' Infantry Division. To the south-west was the XII Battaglione bersaglieri with two companies of German 3.7cm anti-tank guns and the I Gruppo of the 132° Reggimento artiglieria, equipped with 75/27 Mod. 1911 guns. To the north-west was Maggiore Pasquali's 105/28 Mod. 1913 gun group and Capitano Priore's lorry-mounted 102/35 Mod. 1914 gun group. Further to the north-west were the 146 M13/40s of the 132° Reggimento fanteria carrista. Late on 18 November, a company of 16 tanks of the VII Battaglione carri and a battery of 75/27 Mod. 1911 guns deployed to Bir el Diema, 12km south-east of Bir el Gobi, awaiting signs of the British. The 'Ariete' Armoured Division had up to 162 L3/35 tankettes of the 32° Reggimento fanteria carrista, though many did not function and would not be deployed in the battle.

On 18 November the three brigades of 7th Armoured Division advanced in a semicircle towards Tobruk. Sidi Rezegh airfield was captured by 22 Armoured Brigade, cutting the Axis supply lines and thereby forcing the German and Italian tank formations to fight for it. The Allied infantry advanced, intending to squeeze the enemy between themselves and the armour. At this time, 22 Armoured Brigade had 166 Crusaders supported by the eight 25-pdrs of C Bty 4 RHA, a 2-pdr anti-tank troop of 102 Anti-Tank Regiment and an infantry company. Each regiment of 22 Armoured Brigade had a headquarters squadron with four Crusaders and two close-support Crusaders, plus three squadrons, each with a headquarters troop of two Crusaders and two close-support Crusaders and four troops each of three tanks. The other brigades were 4 Armoured Brigade (M3 Stuart) and 7 Armoured Brigade (older cruisers and Crusaders). While 7 Support Group was ordered to follow 7 Armoured Brigade, 22 Armoured Brigade would make the widest sweep around the Italian defences to get to Tobruk. An Allied infantry division was supposed to occupy Bir el Gobi once the 'Ariete' Armoured Division was defeated; in the event, 22 Armoured Brigade was told not to wait for infantry support and would attack without them.

The Allied attack began at 0600hrs: 2 RGH had H Sqn leading, F Sqn on the right and G Sqn on the left. The British tanks moved through the breaches in the wire made before the attack had begun and by 1000hrs reached the petrol dumps established on 17 November. By the end of 18 November, 2 RGH leaguered 120km from where the Allied attack commenced. The British now knew the Italians were at Bir el Gobi, a short distance to the north-west.

At 0700hrs on 19 November, 2 RGH got going again. At this stage, 22 Armoured Brigade had 140 Crusaders operational. Strong south-easterly winds threw up clouds of sand, added to by the dust generated by the tanks' tracks. The company of 16 tanks with a battery of 75/27 Mod. 1911 guns thrown forward by Maretti would be the first to engage 2 RGH. Soon after 0930hrs, they approached G Sqn. Lieutenant-Colonel Birley ordered Major Douglas M. Reinhold's H Sqn to go round to attack these Italian tanks. The M13/40s changed direction and H Sqn was fired upon. The VII Battaglione carri's 3ᵃ Compagnia, led by Capitano Arturo Zanolla with Tenente Pietro Pracca assisting him, lost at least three tanks and seven damaged. Pracca's tank was bogged down and could not get away. Zanolla's tank was hit and his body was brought back by the others; Tenente Umberto Sobrero and Tenente Benito Fabbri suffered the same fate. Elements of the VII Battaglione carri's 2ᵃ Compagnia, led by Tenente Gian Luigi Bossi, fought alongside the 3ᵃ Compagnia. Bossi was wounded during the engagement.

Lieutenant T. Elder Jones, of H Sqn, described this first engagement (Pitman 1950: 17). Two troops were with Reinhold and two others 800yd (732m) back. Reinhold approached the enemy behind a rise then went 90 degrees to the left for 1.6km. Shells began bursting among the Crusaders. The 16 M13/40s had turned off from G Sqn and headed towards them. Jones was with the second-line troops. His aerial was knocked out so he had no contact with the squadron commander, and decided to move up to the front. The dust limited Jones's lines of sight. When it dissipated he noticed an Italian tank 400yd (366m) away. McRae, his gunner, fired twice and set the Italian tank on fire. Jones's Crusader then had a track hit and Jones ordered his driver to go in circles, hoping that remaining in motion would reduce the chance of an Italian round striking the tank. The track would not budge, so Jones ordered smoke to be fired and the engine to be kept running. A hit near the smoke mortar had made it unserviceable, however. Jones opened the hatch to look around. A shell burst right by the front of the hull just after he got back inside. He kept swinging the periscope and suddenly spotted an Italian tank 50yd (46m) away through a patch of smoke. McRae swung the Crusader around but was not fast enough, as two hits on the left side knocked out the engine. The petrol did not ignite. At this point, 4 CLY was firing from long range and Jones thought they had hit his engine (Pitman 1950: 19). With the Crusader's engine out, McRae had to use the hand traverse to shift the turret to the right. He managed to hit the enemy tank. Jones then heard an engine sound and ordered the gunner to traverse the turret to the left, but the traverse was too slow. A shell hit the junction of the left and front turret plates and penetrated, killing McRae. The loader was wounded as was Jones, who now ordered the survivors to bale out. Three other knocked-out tanks, those of 2nd Lieutenant Geoffrey T. Honeysett, Sergeant Clifford J. Woodger and 2nd Lieutenant Geoffrey Gordon-Creed, could be seen. Italian crewmen approached to take Jones prisoner, but Trooper Lee grabbed the turret machine gun and drove them away, allowing Jones to evade capture.

OPPOSITE
This map shows the encounter at Bir el Gobi on 19 November 1941.

Bir el Gobi, 19 November 1941

(1) **1030–1200hrs:** H Sqn, 2 RGH, encounters the 3ª Compagnia, VII Battaglione carri, 132º Reggimento fanteria carrista, at Bir el Diema. H Sqn loses four Crusaders, 3ª Compagnia three M13/40s destroyed and others damaged. The 1ª Compagnia, VII Battaglione carri, is sent south to help extricate the 3ª Compagnia.

(2) **1200–1230hrs:** G Sqn, 2 RGH, attacks the III Battaglione armi d'accompagnamento, which is not yet properly entrenched. Initially successful, some Crusaders drive north past Bir el Gobi while others get stuck among Italian gun positions.

(3) **1230hrs:** F Sqn, 2 RGH, attacks the V Battaglione bersaglieri, which is supported by lorry-mounted 102/35 Mod. 14 guns. The British tankers suffer losses and withdraw, deciding to bypass the Italian positions.

(4) **1230–1330hrs:** 4 CLY attacks positions of the XII Battaglione bersaglieri. A Sqn is stopped by artillery fire. B Sqn, ordered on a wide sweep, has a better time. C Sqn attacks the Italian left flank where lorries are located; 102/35 guns deployed among the lorries destroy nearly half of A Sqn's tanks.

(5) **1300–1330hrs:** The 132º Reggimento fanteria carrista counter-attacks, first with elements of the VII Battaglione carri and then with the VIII Battaglione carri. The 2ª Compagnia, VII Battaglione carri, is sent east. The VIII Battaglione carri is ordered east and north-east.

(6) **1330–1500hrs:** F Sqn and G Sqn, 2 RGH, have difficulty holding their positions.

(7) **1530hrs:** Committed to assisting 2 RGH, 3 CLY manages to deter some Italian armour, knocking out a platoon's worth of M13/40s.

(8) **1600–1630hrs:** 2 RGH withdraws when the IX Battaglione carri, committed on a wide sweeping manoeuvre, threatens to encircle the British tankers.

(9) **1730hrs:** 22 Armoured Brigade withdraws.

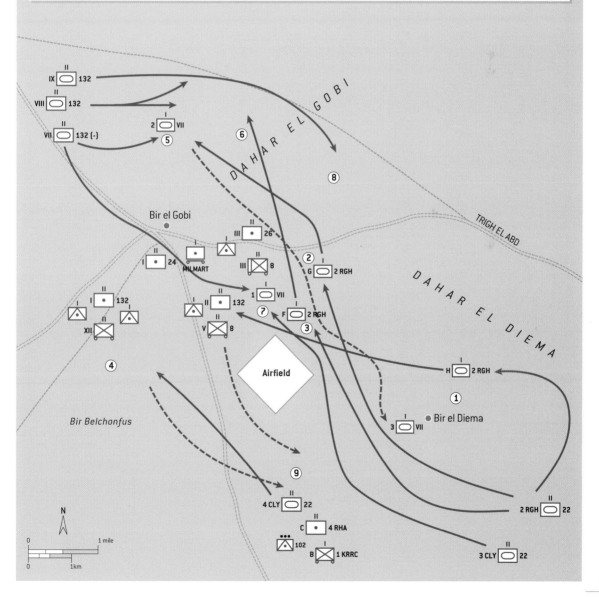

PREVIOUS PAGES

After 2nd Lieutenant Gordon-Creed's Crusader had a track shot off, he continued to circle on the other track and knocked out two M13/40s at point-blank range. His tank was hit again on the turret, and the gunner and radio operator were wounded. The other crew members got them to safety and went back to the tank later, repairing it by the next morning. Despite these losses, Major Reinhold, OC H Sqn, 2 RGH, reported he had knocked out six Italian tanks.

Crusaders move through the desert in battle formation. Note the identifying pennants on the aerial. During the battle of Bir el Gobi, the units of 22 Armoured Brigade were deployed in echelon and could offer one another only limited support. While 2 RGH was on the right, 4 CLY was behind on the left, with A Sqn leading, B Sqn on the left and C Sqn on the right; 3 CLY was to the rear of 4 CLY. Allied infantry were lacking, with 7 Support Group following 7 Armoured Brigade to Sidi Rezegh. The support brigade was ordered to Bir el Gobi late on 18 November; this was not early enough. (The Tank Museum 2260-C4)

At midday, H Sqn could not be rallied, so regimental headquarters ordered G Sqn to lead with F Sqn on the left. G Sqn managed to attack the III Battaglione armi d'accompagnamento successfully as the *Bersaglieri* support battalion had not had time to entrench properly, the British tankers shooting-up numerous lorries. The Crusaders approached enemy positions and found Italians ready to surrender, but the tanks were unable to deal with them and pressed on. Italian crews remained with their guns because they could not surrender. Some Crusaders got stuck amid the Italian positions. At ranges of 200m or less, the 47/32 Mod. 1935 anti-tank guns and 75/27 Mod. 1906 guns inflicted serious damage on the Crusaders. Captain J. Paterson's tank was immobilized; hit multiple times, it caught fire and the crew had to surrender. An M13/40 platoon from the IX Battaglione carri was ordered to support the *Bersaglieri* and was dealt with by G Sqn and H Sqn. Elsewhere, F Sqn approached V Battaglione bersaglieri and was halted by fire from infantry in better entrenched positions supported by the 102/35 Mod. 1914 gun group.

The commanders of 4 CLY and 2 RGH communicated the situation to the brigade commander. The attack was now to be focused on the Italian right. The Crusaders did not withdraw beyond the range of the Italian guns before launching this new attack, meaning the tanks were targeted while deploying and could not respond. As 4 CLY approached the positions of XII Battaglione bersaglieri, also not properly entrenched, A Sqn was stopped by artillery fire; B Sqn ordered on a wide sweep, had a better time, going around the enemy's right, while C Sqn attacked the enemy's left flank where lorries were located. Two platoons of C Sqn got through the enemy trenches, though again could not accept the surrender of Italians. Lieutenant P.G.C. Somerville's No. 1 Platoon was lost, destroyed by the 102/35 Mod. 1914 guns, mistakenly thought to be lorries. The commander of No. 2 Platoon, Lieutenant J.S. Hankey, was also killed. Major William A.B. Onslow, known as Viscount Cranley, commanding C Sqn, overran an Italian anti-tank gun about to target the Crusader of Lieutenant Count J. de Bendern, the No. 3 Platoon commander, at a range of 70yd (64m). Cranley destroyed the Italian gun, but lost a track; he was rescued at the end of the day. The command of 8° Reggimento bersaglieri were surrounded, but managed to get back to supporting positions because the British lacked infantry to stop them.

At this point, 2 RGH noticed a large force of Italian tanks to the north. Ordered to engage them, G Sqn led while F Sqn offered protection on the right flank. They ran into the advance of 100 M13/40s sent in battalion groups by Maretti. The 102/35 Mod. 1914 guns opened up in support of the Italian attack. The British described the

Personnel of the 'Ariete' Armoured Division during Operation *Crusader*, November 1941. (ullstein bild/ullstein bild via Getty Images)

enemy as being deployed in a tight box, halting at 2,740m to engage and then closing to 1,830m to fire again (Pitman 1950: 14). The Italian 47/32 tank gun was more accurate at long range than the British tank-mounted 2-pdr. Only at 1530hrs did 3 CLY deploy to support 4 CLY and 2 RGH.

Tenente Roberto Rosselli, a platoon commander in the VIII Battaglione carri, could see the shapes of the Crusaders disappear and then reappear through the clouds of sand as this new attack commenced (Rebora 2021: 50). He saw a Crusader burning, hit in the engine, to his right. The bursts of igniting ammunition could be distinguished among the flames. A hatch opened, though nobody emerged from it. Large patches of fuel and oil formed around other motionless Crusaders, portending a similar happening. Initially, the clouds of sand aided Rosselli, but when the sand dispersed he found the enemy to be to the side and not to the front, at close range. The British wrought havoc, setting many ablaze. The Italian tanks' ammunition began to run out and Rosselli radioed the battalion headquarters, asking to be resupplied. Tenente Enrico Serra tackled this task and soon a Lancia lorry commanded by Sottotenente Agostinetti could be seen. The hatches were opened and the gun ammunition was unloaded. Rosselli engaged the British again even though a hit in the turret immobilized his gun. He ordered his driver, Sergente Giuseppe Zuccon, to withdraw. For some reason Rosselli decided to dismount and make his way to Tenente Lojodice's tank, perhaps to pass on a message because the radio was not working. Rosselli was hit by shrapnel from a 2-pdr round on the leg. Lojodice spotted him and got him to cling to the hatches of the turret. Another 2-pdr round hit a hatch, slamming it against Rosselli's head.

Tenente Serra highlighted the calmness of Tenente colonnello Maretti, who stood by his staff car issuing orders, despite the enemy rounds whistling by. Serra's VIII Battaglione carri led the Italian counter-attack. An enemy round hit Serra's command tank, knocking off an exhaust pipe; another blow made the tank bounce. A round had hit the turret, and splinters wounded Capitano Casale De Bustis y Figueroa on the head. The gun no longer worked. Despite such losses, the VIII Battaglione carri was

M13/40s in motion with hatches open. Tenente Angelo Murer, the commander of 1ª Compagnia, VII Battaglione carri, was sent forward during the early afternoon of 19 November. Tenente Michele Girardi, a platoon commander, noticed Murer's tank turning back (Rebora 2021: 46). Murer had been struck by a shot that was deflected off the upper hatch, killing him while he was exposed and in the process of directing his tanks. (The Tank Museum 3182-D2)

reinforced by the IX Battaglione carri, deployed on a turning manoeuvre while the other tank battalions engaged the British frontally.

Able to escape because of the Crusader's superior speed, 2 RGH ordered a withdrawal at 1630hrs. Having had to abandon his immobilized tank, Birley was wounded while sitting on his other regimental headquarters tank. A total of 30 Crusaders had been lost, though ten of these would be retrieved by the next morning. The regiment suffered 51 casualties, including 25 captured. Next morning, the 19 tanks still working formed a squadron commanded by Major William A.B. Trevor. During the engagement, 4 CLY had lost eight tanks, 3 CLY four tanks. In the event, 22 Armoured Brigade abandoned the sweeping manoeuvre and was sent north-east to assist 7 Armoured Brigade near Sidi Rezegh.

The Italians lost 12 officers and 193 enlisted men dead, wounded or missing. The officers were from the 132º Reggimento fanteria carrista. Of seven tank company commanders who fought in the battle, four were killed and one wounded. The *Bersaglieri* had nine dead, 38 wounded and 17 missing. The artillery had eight

British prisoners of war at Bir el Gobi. Most prisoners were tank crew-members who had successfully baled out. (Mondadori via Getty Images)

wounded. Altogether, 34 M13/40s were destroyed and 15 damaged; four 75/27 Mod. 1911 guns and eight 47/32 Mod. 1935 anti-tank guns were lost. The battle and the continued presence of the 'Ariete' Armoured Division stopped the British from concentrating their tanks to face the German armour.

An abandoned Crusader at Bir el Gobi, photographed during the winter after the battle. (The Picture Art Collection/Alamy Stock Photo)

THE BATTLE OF GAZALA

On 29 May 1942, the 'Ariete' Armoured Division was deployed on Deir el Aslagh and Haigias es Sidra; the latter feature dominated the Trigh Capuzzo desert track. The Italian tankers guarded the eastern front of the Cauldron. The VII, IX and X Battaglioni carri, supported by two Semovente 75/18 self-propelled-gun groups and artillery, helped the Italian infantry hold positions. Generale di divisione Giuseppe de Stefanis, commander of the 'Ariete' Armoured Division, constructed positions on Aslagh Ridge, with 47/32 Mod. 1935 anti-tank guns occupying the first line, backed up by 88/55 guns and the lorry-mounted 90/53 guns. The guns pointed eastwards; the tanks took up positions further back with the ridge in front. The 15. Panzer-Division and the 90. leichte Division were also within the Cauldron. The British box manned by 150 Infantry Brigade was holding out despite repeated Axis efforts to storm the position.

Early on 30 May, 9th Queen's Royal Lancers (9 QRL), 2 Armoured Brigade, got onto a ridge east of Aslagh Ridge. About 5km away they could see a line of 35 enemy tanks spaced 27m apart. The Italians had deployed 132° Reggimento fanteria carrista's VIII and IX Battaglioni carri supported by a battery of Semovente 75/18 self-propelled guns and a battery of 75/27 Mod. 1911 guns on the right of the Italian line. The

British attack landed on the IX Battaglione carri: 9 QRL was out front, with B Sqn in the lead, C Sqn on the left and A Sqn on the right; the Queen's Bays followed with 16 tanks. The 10th Royal Hussars (Prince of Wales's Own) had only three tanks by then. Many Axis anti-tank guns situated by derelict tanks took a toll on the Crusaders and Grants. The close-support Crusaders laid down smoke and the tanks withdrew; 17 tanks would make it out.

A Sqn, 3 CLY, plus another Crusader squadron from 2 RGH were sent to support 2 Armoured Brigade to try again, supported by 60 guns. Smoke was supposed to be used at 1520hrs, with the British attack beginning at 1530hrs. The guns commenced firing smoke at 1510hrs, ten minutes earlier than planned, and by the time the attack commenced the smoke was gone. The attack had the same consequences. At this point 9 QRL had ten tanks left – six Grants and four knocked-about Crusaders. The Grants would be sent to the Queen's Bays and the regiment was withdrawn. The guns of the 'Ariete' Armoured Division had again probably done most damage. The artillery regiment of 'Ariete' was equipped with two groups of 75/27 Mod. 1911 guns, a group of 105/28 Mod. 1913 guns, two groups of Semovente 75/18 self-propelled guns, a group of 90/53 guns plus a group of 88/55 guns. On 1 June, German armour supported by Italian infantry successfully stormed the box defended by 150 Infantry Brigade.

On 5 June, Eighth Army commenced another effort to destroy Axis units within the Cauldron. The Axis positions on the Aslagh and Sidra ridges were attacked by 7 RTR, 42 RTR and elements of 1st and 7th Armoured divisions along with 201 Guards Motor Brigade Group, 9 Indian Infantry Brigade and 10 Indian Infantry Brigade. On Sidra Ridge, the Italian lorry-mounted 90/53 guns again caused damage to British tanks. On Aslagh Ridge, the Indian brigades attacked to neutralize Axis anti-tank guns, but found the enemy positions to be empty; the Axis forces had withdrawn to a second ridge close by. The British armour refused to support the Indian brigades' attack on this position. The 8° Reggimento bersaglieri held on to part of the second ridge. Rommel launched his own armoured counter-attack on the same

BELOW LEFT

A 2-pdr Crusader at Agedabia, 1942. A track link has broken and the idler wheels no longer hold the track links in place. An Axis round has hit and caused the tank to burn. (Süddeutsche Zeitung Photo/Alamy Stock Photo)

BELOW RIGHT

Soldiers gather on the hull of a Crusader III. (The Tank Museum 4379-E4)

day, destroying many of the attacking Allied formations. On the morning of 12 June, British armour tried to envelop a battalion of 8° Reggimento bersaglieri supported by 132° Reggimento fanteria carrista's VIII Battaglione carri on Point 158. When M3 Grants and Crusaders attacked on each flank, the Italians targeted the M3 Grants and the attack collapsed. On 12 June 1942, the 'Ariete' Armoured Division's destruction of British armour was mentioned in dispatches.

On 16 June, Rommel ordered a general advance to surround Tobruk; this was achieved by 18 June. The 'Littorio' Armoured Division was then committed, with only two tank battalions (XII and LI) and two *Bersaglieri* battalions, to counter British attempts to get through to Tobruk. No efforts would be made to lift the siege.

On 24 June, the 'Littorio' Armoured Division reached the Egyptian frontier with sufficient fuel for only another 60km, but had orders to move 120km in order to surround Mersa Matruh. The seizure of a British depot helped the Axis supply situation. During the night of 29/30 June, 'Littorio' advanced through difficult terrain south-east of Fuka and encountered British tanks at dawn: 21 M14/41s attacked eight tanks, half of them Grants. The British withdrew after inflicting many losses, including Tenente colonnello Salvatore Zappalà, the commander of the LI Battaglione carri, who died at the head of his battalion.

On 3 July, the 'Ariete' Armoured Division, with two lorry-borne *Bersaglieri* battalions, six artillery groups and one battalion's worth of M14/41s, was attacked by 2 Armoured Brigade, 1st Armoured Division and 4 New Zealand Infantry Brigade. The 'Trieste' Motorized Division failed to maintain contact with 'Ariete'; 28 Italian guns were lost and only eight Italian tanks would be operational after the engagement. The same day on Ruweisat Ridge, the 'Littorio' Armoured Division's tank strength was depleted by other armour units of 1st Armoured Division.

An M13/40 of the 1° Plotone, unknown company, IV Battaglione carri, 133° Reggimento fanteria carrista. By the beginning of March 1942, the 'Ariete' Armoured Division had 101 medium tanks, the 'Littorio' Armoured Division 64. Before the battle of Gazala began on 26 May 1942, 'Ariete' had 193 medium tanks, including 70 M14/41s, and 'Littorio' 157, including 39 M13/40s. (The Tank Museum 3182-B6)

CRUSADER I GUN SIGHT

5
10
15

4
8
12

GUN

MG

This single sight for both the 2-pdr gun and the Besa machine gun was used as the speeds of the two types of shot were similar. The range markings illustrate hundreds of yards. The magnification was 1.9×. The Mk 30 sighting telescope was used. The gunner found the graticule could block the target at ranges greater than 1,000yd (914m). An illuminated graticule for use in dim light conditions was not provided.

M13/40 GUN SIGHT

The telescope for the gunner located on the right of the turret had 1.25× magnification and horizon sector of 30 degrees, and was graduated for a range of 1,200m for the main gun and 900m for the machine gun. The crosshairs were moved by a knob on the top of the graticule box. The gun could be operated by a foot pedal or manually.

THE SECOND BATTLE OF EL ALAMEIN

The First Battle of El Alamein had seen a less mobile battle being fought because the British had withdrawn to a 55km-wide line between the Qattara Depression and the sea. When the Second Battle of El Alamein commenced on 23 October 1942, the east–west ridge lines running through the Allied defences would again be the focus of operations for Montgomery as he would first attempt to destroy the Axis infantry and then advance the Allied armour formations. To this end, 51st Highland Division and 2nd New Zealand Division attacked the Axis infantry – four battalions, two Italian (62° Reggimento fanteria) and two German (Infanterie-Regiment 382) – occupying these positions, entrenched in gun pits with thick minefields to their front between Miteiriya Ridge and Kidney Ridge; the Allied armour would flow through the gaps in the minefields. The 'Littorio' Armoured Division occupied positions on the northern part of the line, the 'Ariete' Armoured Division positions on the southern part of the line. Montgomery focused his attention on the north.

The LI Battaglione carri, stationed furthest north with a *Panzergrenadier* battalion, was attacked by 26 Australian Infantry Brigade. Further south, the IV Battaglione carri was stationed on Point 33, with a Panzer battalion from Panzer-Regiment 8 nearby and a *Panzergrenadier* battalion on Kidney Ridge. A self-propelled-gun group was also close by with a 100/17 gun group, 88/55 gun group and *Bersaglieri* battalion. They would predominantly face the Highlanders and New Zealanders. To the south, the XII Battaglione carri was located near Whiska Ridge, south of Kidney Ridge, with a Panzer battalion from Panzer-Regiment 8. A self-propelled-gun group and 75/27 Mod. 1911 gun group stood close by. A *Panzergrenadier* battalion was also deployed in the area.

The first line of Axis infantry in front of Whiska Ridge soon needed Capitano Costanzo Preve's XII Battaglione carri (133° Reggimento carri fanteria), supported by a group of Semovente 75/18 self-propelled guns, to deploy to plug the gaps. Moving through the channels made in the Axis minefields, 8 Armoured Brigade (10th Armoured Division) had bunched up. Also in the queue were 9 Armoured Brigade and 24 Armoured Brigade; these formations had little room for manoeuvre. Serving alongside the Nottinghamshire Yeomanry and 3 RTR in 8 Armoured Brigade, the Staffordshire Yeomanry sent Major Charles R. Farquhar's Crusader-equipped C Sqn on ahead. Farquhar lost five Crusaders to mines and four to enemy guns early on 24 October. Then, together with a battalion from Panzer-Regiment 8, the M14/41s mounted a counter-attack. The subsequent withdrawal of 8 Armoured Brigade to Miteiriya Ridge was probably prompted not by the action of the Axis armour, however, but by the fact that the enemy anti-tank gun line was undefeated.

The British order for 25 October was to occupy Whiska Ridge by attacking during the hours of darkness. The Nottinghamshire Yeomanry was late getting through the minefield, however, and only 3 RTR and Staffordshire Yeomanry would be in position. The British attack was decimated by anti-tank guns. Consolidating its remaining tanks into a composite squadron, the Staffordshire Yeomanry helped 9 Armoured Brigade defend Miteiriya Ridge from an Axis armoured sortie late on 25 October. On 28 October the Allied infantry defended positions so 9 Armoured Brigade could be

Pictured near the Qattara Depression during the autumn of 1942, these M13/40s have sandbags bolstering their protection. (Atlantic-Press/ullstein bild via Getty Images)

brought out of the line to get ready for Montgomery's next operation, Operation *Supercharge*. The Staffordshire Yeomanry's Crusader squadron was brought up to strength though the regiment's other two squadrons had only 16 tanks between them. The Staffordshire Yeomanry's losses would be limited during Operation *Supercharge*, with four of its Crusaders knocked out by anti-tank guns or stray mines.

During the morning of 25 October, 9 Armoured Brigade's 3rd The King's Own Hussars was between Miteiriya Ridge and Whiska Ridge: A Sqn had two 6-pdr Crusaders and four 2-pdr Crusaders; B Sqn had seven Shermans, three Grants and one 6-pdr Crusader; and C Sqn had seven Shermans, seven Grants and one 6-pdr Crusader. During the morning, the Crusaders had a bad time going through the minefields and A Sqn and B Sqn had to be amalgamated because of losses. Some M14/41s could be seen, though the Axis forces used anti-tank guns on Whiska Ridge to do the damage and did not attack with armour. The brigade withdrew to the safety of Miteiriya Ridge by the end of the day. No further attacks could be made and on 27 October 9 Armoured Brigade withdrew to get ready for Operation *Supercharge*; 24 Armoured Brigade was not withdrawn, though, and was placed under command of 1st Armoured Division.

Further north, 1st Armoured Division had deployed 7 Motor Brigade with 2 Armoured Brigade towards Kidney Ridge on 25 October. The IV and LI Battaglione carri and one battalion of Panzer-Regiment 8 attacked 2 Armoured Brigade on Miteiriya Ridge. Altogether, 30 per cent of Italian tanks were hit. Claiming 18 Axis tanks knocked out, 2 Armoured Brigade also lost heavily, with only 120 out of 161 tanks operational at the end of the day.

Campini described the engagement (Campini 2015b: 99–100). On 24 October, the IV Battaglione carri, commanded by Tenente colonnello Rocco Casamassima, withstood Allied artillery bombardment while waiting to launch a counter-attack; the Italian tankers had shifted to protect the 88/55 guns. On 25 October, infantry from 51st (Highland) Division attacked positions in front of Point 33, near Kidney Ridge, while 7 Motor Brigade attempted to outflank the Axis position by going around the enemy's right. Deploying from the north, the LI Battaglione carri attacked along with the IV Battaglione carri and the battalion from Panzer-Regiment 8. Campini described a quick and bloody fight because the stationary enemy had a choice of targets and targeted them from the flank. The German tanks did not coordinate properly and the Italians attacked on a 1,000m frontage; 18 M14/41s were soon lost. Casamassima was wounded and evacuated and Capitano Vittorio Piccinini, the 3ª Compagnia commander, was killed, as was Tenente Mario Ronga, the commander of the 2ª Compagnia.

Campini thought the attack was a mistake (Campini 2015b: 99–100). He had to take command of the IV Battaglione carri after this engagement. Each company was now organized with two platoons of five tanks. Campini determined to deploy his battalion with one company forward and the other two back because the losses they suffered could be partly explained by being targeted from the flank. He also shifted closer to the German Panzer battalion, though at dusk on 25 October a courier brought an order from 133° Reggimento fanteria carrista headquarters sending him to Point 33 again. Campini checked on his wounded first and found some in the German medical half-tracks. He noted the lack of an Italian armoured vehicle capable of evacuating the wounded; his unit only had a lorry. Luckily, Dr Schmidt, a battalion doctor with the Germans, was able to help out. The LI Battaglione carri also suffered losses, including the commander Capitano Tito Puddu, who was mortally wounded, and Capitano Caraccio, a company commander.

Late on 26 October, supplies of ammunition, water and fuel arrived, brought forward by Tenente Greppi. Two platoons led by Tenenti Morini and Colonna aided German *Panzergrenadiere*. Campini established supply dumps: 180 litres of fuel allowed 8 hours' running time for one tank. Fuel containers stowed on the rear of the hull were now of limited utility because shrapnel had punctured many of them. Campini noted that his tanks had a total of 105 rounds of ammunition early on 27 October. By that time a self-propelled-gun battery commanded by Capitano Sciortino joined up with the IV Battaglione carri, still near the 88/55 gun group. With these, Campini's battalion managed to contain 7 Motor Brigade near Kidney Ridge. The self-propelled guns destroyed an Allied anti-tank battery at a range of about 400m as it attempted to deploy.

The 'Littorio' Armoured Division and the Germans had faced British infantry from 7 Motor Brigade, who had entrenched on positions to the south-west and north-west of Kidney Ridge on the morning of 27 October; defended by a battalion of German motorized infantry, the ridge would later be assaulted by troops of 51st (Highland) Division during the night. Meanwhile, 7 Motor Brigade's 2nd Battalion, The Rifle Brigade, dug in to the south-west of the ridge with 16 6-pdr anti-tank guns on soft ground. An Axis counter-attack from the south conducted by the XII Battaglione carri, a DLIV Gruppo Semovente, I./PzRgt 8 and a battalion of German anti-tank guns failed when confronted by the 6-pdrs of 7 Motor Brigade, supported by units of 24 Armoured Brigade. 'Littorio' lost 16 tanks and four 75/18 self-propelled guns on 27 October. Allied infantry and anti-tank guns, rather than tanks, had stopped the Axis armoured counter-attack. The Axis lacked the necessary infantry and artillery support to attack the outpost and tried to do so primarily with armour.

M3 Grant tanks in Libya, 1942. Major-General McCreery noted after the battle of Gazala that the Grant was slow and could not work well with Crusaders or Stuarts (Knight 2015: 72). Grants could cover only 16 miles (26km) in two hours. Crusaders needed to be run slowly when operating with Grants and this caused the Crusaders' engines to overheat. The Crusader was not capable of holding ground, however, because it was not robust enough to stand up to high-explosive rounds compared to the Grant. (Geoffrey John Keating/Imperial War Museums via Getty Images)

On 28 October, Campini was ordered to move from Point 33 to a position north-west of El Wishka to support a battalion of *Panzergrenadiere*. The Germans had created reference points made from petrol drums and marked them on maps, but the German infantry had left. During the afternoon of 29 October, German armour from Panzer-Regiment 5 appeared and Campini had direct communication at last. The XII Battaglione carri and the self-propelled guns of the DLIV Gruppo Semovente were also told to move to El Wishka. Then Campini received new orders, to guard artillery batteries until the 21. Panzer-Division, deploying from the south, reached the location. These artillery batteries were close to the 88/55 gun group and Campini discovered that the latter had been captured by the enemy. He counter-attacked the positions around Point 33 and recaptured the 88/55 guns; 350 Allied soldiers were taken prisoner by accompanying German infantry. Campini was then ordered to protect the 100/17 guns commanded by Capitano Lusiana before taking up positions with a *Bersaglieri* battalion near Point 28. By 1 November, the XII Battaglione carri was moved up, along with the DLIV Gruppo Semovente, to operate with the other two tank battalions from the 'Littorio' Armoured Division.

Also on 28 October, 1st Armoured Division had to be replaced by 10th Armoured Division, meaning that 133 Lorried Infantry Brigade took the place of 7 Motor Brigade. This swapping of formations while engaged on the front lines caused some confusion. Axis counter-attacks sought to exploit the situation, with a battalion from 133 Lorried Infantry Brigade losing 400 men when attacked by elements of the 'Littorio' Armoured Division and German motorized infantry; this was probably the encounter Campini described.

The Germans then deployed 21. Panzer-Division elements with 132° Reggimento fanteria carrista's IX Battaglione carri to mount a counter-attack on another section of line near Kidney Ridge. Interception of German signals sent during the morning of 28 October told the British this would happen by the afternoon. As a result, 2 Armoured Brigade was ordered to close up with the infantry. Allied fighters intercepted Axis air support and forced it to return to base. Confronted by an Allied field-artillery barrage and long-range gunnery from Shermans and Grants, the Axis counter-attack was a complete failure.

While the Axis infantry was mostly standing its ground, German and Italian armour could not conduct successful counter-attacks to deal with the Allied forces' penetrations of the Axis line. The Axis forces had only 1½ days of petrol and this hampered their ability to fight a mobile battle. By 28 October, the Axis had 81 German and 196 Italian tanks operational: 129 belonged to the largely uncommitted 'Ariete' Armoured Division. The British could deploy 700 tanks. Montgomery was winning his battle of attrition. On 27 October, he ordered 7th Armoured Division to move north; the division had 70 Grants, 27 Crusaders and 50 Stuarts. This meant the 'Ariete' Armoured Division did not need to stay in the south to keep 7th Armoured Division in check.

On 29 October, the combatants reorganized. Rommel knew he had to withdraw, but would not contemplate beginning the process until Allied troops had breached his line. Montgomery planned an attack, codenamed Operation *Supercharge*, to smash the Axis line. He knew Rommel's fuel shortages were hampering the German commander's ability to use the Axis armour. The Allied focus was again on the front near Kidney Ridge. Tell el Aqqaqir – an observation point situated on the north–south Rahman Track, about 5km north-west of Kidney Ridge – was to be captured. Roughly 80 infantry-support tanks would assist the Allied infantry in their attack on the front line. Then 9 Armoured Brigade would attack the Axis anti-tank line along the Rahman Track. The other armoured brigades would be brought up as needed. Distracted by Australian forces' presence on the coast, Rommel did not think Montgomery would attack on 2 November. Having been informed about the arrival of a fuel ship, the German commander was planning a withdrawal to Fuka, near the Mersa Matruh logistics base, some 80km to the west.

The Allied infantry attack launched early on 2 November completely succeeded; four German and Italian battalions defending the line could not repulse the attack of two Allied brigades supported by the infantry-support tanks. After conducting a 16km approach march through the darkness and dust clouds and facing landmines and Axis artillery fire, only 94 tanks of 9 Armoured Brigade reached the brigade's jumping-off point by morning. The delay meant the main Allied attack happened in daylight.

This column of M13/40 tanks near El Alamein is led by a company commander. On 26 October, the Axis forces successfully used their armoured groups to contain further Allied attacks on Kidney Ridge and on El Wishka to the south. Elsewhere, Allied infantry attacks on the main Axis line during the night of 25/26 October forced the Germans and Italians to withdraw to a series of hastily prepared positions further back. (ullstein bild via Getty Images)

Photographed on 5 November 1942, these Sherman tanks of C Sqn, 9 QRL, are serving in 2 Armoured Brigade, 1st Armoured Division. When Operation *Lightfoot* commenced on 23 October, 8 Armoured Brigade had 33 2-pdr Crusaders, 88 Grants or Shermans and 12 Crusader IIIs. This number was eroded by mines and fire from enemy anti-tank guns on the morning of 24 October as the British tanks moved through the gaps in the minefields made by engineers. When they got to Miteiriya Ridge, Axis anti-tank guns targeted the British tanks on the crest. (Sergeant Len Chetwyn/ Imperial War Museums via Getty Images)

The Crusaders of A Sqn, 3 Hussars, took the lead, but landmines and enemy artillery meant nearly 50 per cent of the squadron could not continue. The infantry company accompanying the Crusader squadron was wiped out. When they got to the Rahman Track, the Allied tanks made a large silhouette. They were operating among the forward lighter guns of the German anti-tank line. By the end of 2 November, 3 Hussars had only eight tanks operational. The Royal Wiltshire Yeomanry (24 Grants or Shermans) and Warwickshire Yeomanry (24 Grants or Shermans and 16 Crusaders) had accompanied 3 Hussars; these units would also be down to eight tanks each by the day's end.

The British found 35 German and Italian anti-tank guns destroyed. With 9 Armoured Brigade having not reached the Rahman Track, 8 Armoured Brigade and 2 Armoured Brigade had to join the attack, with 7 Motor Brigade occupying a central position. The Germans launched the 21. Panzer-Division from the north; 7 Motor Brigade had managed to form a gun line and with the support of 2 Armoured Brigade and 8 Armoured Brigade, thwarted the German attack, which was supported by those Italian tanks that were still operational.

Tenente colonnello Giuseppe Bonini, the commander of 133º Reggimento fanteria carrista, who was wounded, stated that by 1000hrs, a wave of British armour had descended on his XII and LI Battaglione carri, supported by the DLIV Gruppo Semovente (Campini 2015b: 115). North of Point 33, the LI Battaglione carri was surrounded and wiped out, as was the 2ª Bateria of the DLIV Gruppo Semovente. South-west of Point 28, the XII Battaglione carri suffered nearly the same fate; its commander, Capitano Costanzo Preve, was wounded. The IV Battaglione carri was initially supported by a German tank company, though the Germans soon disappeared when they ran out of ammunition; the company was back by the afternoon.

Campini had a weak company of M14/41s and three self-propelled guns (Campini 2015b: 115). Smoke screens covered the approach of the British tanks. Campini soon

At El Alamein, Italian tanks required the support of self-propelled guns like this Semovente 75/18 M42, preserved in Bergamo, Italy. The M40 was built on an M13/40 chassis, the M41 on an M14/41 chassis and the M42 on an M15/42 chassis. Up to early September 1943, a total of 288 (60 M40, 162 M41 and 66 M42) were manufactured. (Mannivu/Wikimedia/CC BY-SA 4.0)

had only four tanks and two self-propelled guns left, though he stated that his men had successfully targeted some enemy armour. He noted that the British tanks seemed to be impervious to his shot and would stand 2,000m off, firing up to 30 shots on a single target. By the early evening, Campini had only two tanks operational. Along with Sciortino, he was wounded, though only temporarily stunned by a glancing blow to the head. He had received no orders since dawn. Campini sent Tenente F. Marchegiani, the only officer not wounded, to join up with the German tank company. After getting medical attention, Campini reported the situation to the 'Littorio' Armoured Division's command post, 800m south-west of Tel Alam el Aqqaqir. Campini found his tank crews at the field hospital located near the coast. On 3 November he was evacuated by lorry.

Rommel knew the moment had come to withdraw. On 3 November, the Deutsches Afrikakorps had 24 tanks and the 'Littorio' Armoured Division only 17. Montgomery then committed 7th Armoured Division. Along with 1st Armoured Division, the British tankers would exploit by turning north-west towards the coast when the Allied infantry had seized the Rahman Track. The first British attack would commence late on 3 November, with the intention of hitting the southern portion of the Axis line. The main attack would begin early on 4 November. The Axis withdrawal had in places got going during the night of 3/4 November, though the Axis forces could still target the abandoned Tell el Aqqaqir from afar.

The 'Ariete' Armoured Division took over the role of protecting the German withdrawal. Lacking two *Bersaglieri* battalions because they had stayed in the south, the division retained one *Bersaglieri* battalion, two self-propelled-gun groups and a mixed-gun group with two 90/55 gun batteries and one 88/55 battery. On the morning of 4 November, they took position south of Deir el Murra at the same location through which the British tanks had planned to exploit, to the south of Tell el Aqqaqir.

On 4 November, the Italians formed a gun line against the tanks of 22 Armoured Brigade. By the time of Operation *Supercharge*, the British brigade had 54 Grants, 16 2-pdr Crusaders and ten 6-pdr Crusaders. The Grants belonging to 22 Armoured Brigade stood off and targeted the Italian tanks from 1,500m. The 6-pdr Crusaders could do the same. The tankers of 4 CLY engaged Italian armour west of Dier Murra. The lorry-borne infantry of 7th Armoured Division's 131 Lorried Infantry Brigade were also committed. Some tanks of 4 Armoured Brigade then enveloped the southern end of the Italian line. Despite being nearly surrounded, Tenente colonnello Corrado Mazzara, the commander of the IX Battaglione carri, stated that he withdrew from Bir el Abd during the late afternoon (Campini 2015b: 122). Tenente colonnello Renzo Baldini's XIII Battaglione carri was furthest back from the front line. Mazzara urged him to get out despite communication with Colonnello Paolo Formenti, commander of 132° Reggimento fanteria carrista, being lost. About 30 M13/40s were destroyed by 1530hrs, with about 40 immobilized on the battlefield; another 30 managed to escape. On the British side, 4 CLY reported no tanks lost.

Of the 'Littorio' Armoured Division, by 7 November, only a handful of its assets – two companies of *Bersaglieri*, two 100/17 guns and one company's worth of M14/41s – had managed to escape.

Rommel had tried to deal quickly with enemy breaches of his line in order to stop the British armour from flowing into open space because he did not possess enough strength to form sufficient army reserves. He used large formations to launch counter-attacks, dissipating unit strength against dug-in defences. His artillery could not counter the enemy's batteries because they lacked the range of Allied guns.

Crusaders armed with 2-pdr guns followed by Shermans at El Alamein, 1942. Montgomery had 481 medium tanks for Operation *Supercharge*: 2 Armoured Brigade had 92 Shermans and 68 Crusaders; 22 Armoured Brigade had 54 Grants and 26 Crusaders; 8 Armoured Brigade operated with 47 Crusaders and 62 Grants or Shermans; and 9 Armoured Brigade had 53 Crusaders plus 79 Grants or Shermans. (AFP via Getty Images)

OVERLEAF
This scene shows Tenente Pietro Bruno in combat on 4 November, during the action in which he was fatally wounded. His M14/41 is accompanied by a Semovente 75/18 self-propelled gun. A troop of Crusaders can be seen in the distance.

ANALYSIS

The Crusader was limited by its mechanical issues, which stemmed from the air cleaners being mounted externally, meaning that dust and sand got into the engine, affecting durability. The desert environment was not the cause of the problems, however, as Crusaders in Britain had the same issues. This entailed a high standard of maintenance, as demonstrated by 6 RTR during mid-1941. At first, the small number of Crusaders in service did not place a high strain on base workshops. By the time of Operation *Crusader*, though, the mechanical issues were nearly insurmountable because of compromised overhauls or tanks that had been driven too long. The fitting of an internal air cleaner by base workshops would have eliminated many issues, but this was not done, either because of a lack of understanding about the role played by the external fitting, or an unwillingness to occupy space being used to stow ammunition. The base workshops did not possess the capacity to deal with the issues when deployed to the desert. Spare parts, not new Crusaders, were needed. The priority was quantity, however, including on the factory floor; Crusaders were hurriedly built, sent out with parts not fitted, disembarked incorrectly, and then operated on by workshops lacking in manpower and parts. With a low overhaul mileage, the Crusaders needed to spend time in the workshops anyway. The fitters were overburdened, but the solution at the War Office was to ship more Crusaders out.

When first deployed, the M13/40 and M14/41 were a match for British medium cruiser tanks, judged by their technical attributes. Early on, Italian tank training was not sufficient, though it did get better later with a training centre established in the desert; on-the-job training, made possible because unit cohesion was good, was particularly important. While the 47mm gun was superior to the Crusader's 2-pdr and was capable of penetrating 43mm of armour at 500m, the Italian tanks' armour was inferior to that of the up-armoured Crusader, deployed in numbers from early 1942.

From Gazala onwards, when the Crusaders were accompanied by Grants, the Italian medium tanks could only operate effectively against British armour when defending a gun line. By October 1942, when facing Crusaders with 2-pdrs or 6-pdrs and Shermans operating together, the Italian tanks needed to be protected by a gun line.

The Crusader was not criticized much by its crews. A 6-pdr gun fitted earlier would have helped, as would the provision of 2-pdr APCBC rounds. The stipulation for an 18-tonne tank limited the thickness of armour. The close-support Crusader was much liked, as it could use smoke and high-explosive against enemy anti-tank guns.

Although the Crusader was deployed from June 1941, it would first encounter the M13/40 during Operation *Crusader* later that year. The battle at Bir el Gobi is unique because a brigade completely equipped with Crusaders encountered equivalent Italian opposition that was without German support. The Crusaders had no effective support. When Operation *Crusader* got under way, the British tank brigades operated on divergent axes; they would for the most part fight alone. The support group was posted elsewhere and the infantry battalion assigned to 22 Armoured Brigade was dispersed in company strength to support the armoured regiments. Only one battery of 25-pdrs supported a tank force of brigade strength.

Conversely, the Italians had infantry supported by a substantial number of guns. *Bersaglieri* units had integral anti-tank platoons. Italian combined-arms doctrine stipulated the need for armour to operate with infantry protecting a strong gun line. Lorry-borne heavy artillery could target the Crusaders from long range. Such tactics could be hampered by limited Axis training and rudimentary communications, though with determined leadership at Bir el Gobi they could see off a hurried British tank charge designed to intimidate a supposedly inferior enemy. The British decision

A good side view of the Crusader III. The fact that so many crew are visible and the small intervals between the tanks make it clear this is not a battlefield image. (Keystone/ Getty Images)

to engage was a mistake; 22 Armoured Brigade needed to wait for either the support group or infantry brigade to arrive. The British assumed the Italians would suffer from low morale and surrender, as they had during Operation *Compass*. The official communication about the battle erroneously mentioned encountering German anti-tank guns and PzKpfw IV medium tanks in its attempt to explain the British defeat.

Fortunately for the British, the official lessons-learnt paper for Operation *Crusader* stated that tanks alone could not win battles and that they needed to work closely with infantry and artillery. This led to a decentralized theory of command, based on each brigade operating combined-arms units; this seemed like a positive move, though getting the brigades to cooperate was difficult. The Gazala fighting saw dispersed brigade groups destroyed piecemeal, but Axis losses would be substantial because of the presence of the M3 Grant. Rommel placed his forces on ground the Allied troops had to seize to get through to brigade boxes surrounded by Axis forces. The Axis troops were exposed while fighting in the Cauldron; the British, however, could not coordinate a counter-attack when Rommel was suffering from a lack of supplies. The British armour was used to attack the Axis anti-tank gun line and was then counter-attacked by Axis tanks. The subsequent Allied losses meant a withdrawal to El Alamein and a proper defence line was inevitable. The 'Ariete' Armoured Division played an important role defending the ridges of the Cauldron from 2 Armoured Brigade and 22 Armoured Brigade, mostly equipped with Crusaders. The Italians formed a concealed gun line with armour close by in support.

The Allied attacks on Axis positions during the First Battle of El Alamein in July 1942 were characterized by a mutual distrust between armoured commanders and their infantry counterparts. Army commanders were unable to impose discipline; this changed when Lieutenant-General Montgomery assumed command on 13 August. He brought out many senior officers from Britain that he knew he could work with. Brigade groups were eliminated; the division was the basic fighting unit, bringing together combined arms with the armoured brigade fighting with the motorized brigade; prolific Axis minefields meant armour could not operate without infantry support. The Allied aim was still to destroy the Axis armour, but the method was different. From positions seized by motor battalions, British armour would launch attacks to get to the best ground to withstand counter-attacks from Axis armour. Montgomery wanted to attack the unarmoured portion of an Axis armoured division and ward off enemy tanks with anti-tank guns. A tight control would be exerted over the British armoured brigades to stop attacks on Axis armour before it was sufficiently weakened.

A lack of unit cohesion and training time limited the effect Montgomery's changes made. For example, an infantry brigade was just getting used to a new role as lorried infantry and was then asked to operate with armour. New tanks such as the Sherman and Crusader III had to be issued. Insufficient time to practise the new doctrine forced the plan for Second El Alamein to be changed. No longer would British armour go through breaches in the Axis line torn by the infantry and establish itself on positions on the enemy's lines of communication to fight the armoured battle. Instead the British tankers needed to assist the infantry to destroy the Axis gun line. Enemy minefields thickly sown with anti-tank mines limited the support British tanks could

provide, however. Instead, Axis infantry positions were destroyed piecemeal by Allied infantry attacks during the hours of darkness.

In Rommel's absence, German commanders were too willing to use armour to plug breaches in the line. When Rommel returned from leave he prioritized protecting his gun line. By October 1942, Italian tanks were used to guard gun batteries from Allied infantry attack. By late 1942, however, the Italian medium tanks could not operate independently against British armour. Even when the 'Littorio' Armoured Division worked alongside German armour during the Second Battle of El Alamein, operating together was difficult because of communication problems. Allied motor brigades equipped with 6-pdr guns combined with tank units to deplete the attacking German and Italian armour units near Kidney Ridge.

Rommel was best fighting a mobile battle. The terrain at El Alamein meant Montgomery could fight a less mobile battle. Montgomery's main strength was the ability of his infantry to hold ground supported by artillery. He used them to crumble the Axis line and deplete Rommel's armour. The motor battalions' 6-pdr anti-tank guns could fend off Axis armour, allowing Montgomery's own armour to mount the final, successful attack. Allied armoured units equipped with better tanks in the form of 6-pdr Crusaders and Shermans utilized the combined-arms doctrine needed to win on the battlefield; they exploited when Rommel's armour was weakened. The last of his armour was the 'Ariete' Armoured Division, lacking many of its supporting elements, ordered to delay the Allied pursuit of withdrawing Axis forces. By that stage, the superiority of Montgomery's tanks was so pronounced that 'Ariete' was not able to buy much time and was swept away in its last battle.

A destroyed M13/40 on the battlefield. Campini wrote of problems coordinating with German units during the Second Battle of El Alamein (Campini 2015b: 48). Communication differences hampered Axis cooperation. Campini asked to be kept informed and blamed his German counterparts for a lack of effort. Positioned to the north of Kidney Ridge, the IV and LI Battaglioni carri operated alongside a battalion of Panzer-Regiment 8 and a German motorized-infantry battalion. During the battle, Campini's IV Battaglione carri lost 42 dead, 38 missing and 61 wounded out of a total strength of 202. The missing had probably died when tanks were set alight. (The Tank Museum 0095-B1)

AFTERMATH

By late November 1942, Rommel hastily withdrew to the defences around El Agheila. Montgomery now had longer supply lines and needed to get the rail line and coast road up and running after the Germans had demolished sections. By the middle of December he launched his attack on the Axis positions. The 'Centauro' Armoured Division contributed its tanks to the defences at El Agheila. Formed during June 1942 in Parma, Tenente colonnello G. Fiumi's XIV Battaglione carri had disembarked at Tripoli during October 1942: the 1ª and 2ª compagnie marched to El Agheila, while the 3ª Compagnia was sent to the Mareth Line (a French line of fortifications on the Tunisia/Libya border) further west because Allied forces had landed in French North Africa.

On 13 December, German aircraft detected an Allied column 121km south of the Axis defence line, attempting to envelop Rommel's position. Montgomery planned for infantry to pin Axis forces frontally, with 7th Armoured Division on the northern flank. The Commonwealth infantry was held up by mines, though 8 Armoured Brigade managed to move forwards slightly further south through difficult ground. A strong Axis position with anti-tank ditches and salt marshes was in the way.

On 15 December, 8 Armoured Brigade led the Allied attack, with 2nd New Zealand Division making the wide envelopment to the south. Claiming a total of 22 Allied tanks destroyed, Rommel credited the infantry and guns of Gruppo 'Ariete' for forcing back 8 Armoured Brigade as it attempted to pin Axis positions frontally. Such claims might be exaggerated; the 1ª and 2ª compagnie experienced heavy losses when they conducted a counter-attack. The Axis defences held during the day and were only breached by 131 Infantry Brigade during the hours of darkness. On the morning of 16 December, with Rommel's forces making an orderly withdrawal, 8 Armoured Brigade passed along the coast road. Dispersed after a long journey, the

New Zealanders were not capable of forming a blocking position. Rommel made a further series of withdrawals without major problems and by 22 January his forces were near the Mareth Line. By this date, Montgomery had only just reached Tripoli.

The Mareth Line was not defended by the 'Centauro' Armoured Division, which had been sent further north. Eighth Army deployed its Crusaders during the ensuing battle, mostly against strong infantry and gun positions of the 1ª Armata italiana. During late March, Axis forces made a withdrawal to the Gabes Gap to positions between the impassable salt marshes and the sea. The Allied forces conducted another operation to get through this position on 6 April. The conclusion of the North African campaign in May 1943 marked the end of the Crusader's front-line role.

The organization of Italian armour was different after the North African campaign. The importance of self-propelled guns with heavier main armament meant they would be teamed with M15/42 tanks to operate as joint company formations. Self-propelled guns and towed artillery would also be prioritized. The new organization promoted the use of self-propelled guns to support tanks and stressed the importance of artillery.

Formed on 1 April 1943, by 8 September 1943 the 135ª Divisione cavalleria corazzata 'Ariete' was composed of a cavalry regiment with three tank groups, each with three squadrons. Each squadron had ten Semovente 75/18 M42 self-propelled guns and seven M15/42 tanks. The armoured reconnaissance regiment had one group with 38 AB41 armoured cars, one group with 16 Semovente 47/32 L40 and 12 Semovente 75/18 M42 self-propelled guns and one group with 22 M15/42 medium and 16 L6/40 light tanks. A motorized cavalry regiment included 12 Semovente 75/18 M42 self-propelled guns supporting three lorry-borne infantry groups. The self-propelled artillery regiment had 24 Semovente 105/25 M43 self-propelled guns and 24 75/32 anti-tank guns. The self-propelled anti-tank battalion had 12 Semovente 75/34 guns. The motorized artillery regiment had 36 guns of 100mm calibre or greater and 12 90/53 guns. The division moved to Rome after the fall of Mussolini on 26 July 1943 and fought the Germans on the approaches to the north of the city on 9 September before being dissolved three days later.

ABOVE LEFT

A Crusader III crew of 16/5 Lancers at El Aroussa, Tunisia, prepare for the Allied drive on Tunis, December 1942. Sergeant Elms (seated, top) and Trooper Bates look on as Signalman Bower and Trooper Goddard clean their tank's 6-pdr gun. (G. Loughlin/War Office official photographer/Imperial War Museums via Getty Images)

ABOVE RIGHT

Crusader tanks from 1st Armoured Division pass a German sign indicating a supply of water as they enter El Hamma, Tunisia, on 29 March 1943 following the battle of the Mareth Line. (The Print Collector/Print Collector/Getty Images)

US soldiers inspect a captured M14/41, looking for booby traps. During February 1943, the XIV Battaglione carri fought US forces near Kasserine, alongside the XV and XVII battaglioni carri and other elements of the 'Centauro' Armoured Division. By early March 1943, only 18 M14/41s were operational. 'Centauro' was the focus of US attacks throughout March and was disbanded on 7 April. (Keystone/Getty Images)

Formed on 15 August 1943, the 136ª Divisione legionaria corazzata 'Centauro' incorporated units from the 1ª Divisione corazzata Camicie Nere 'M', Mussolini's personal guard division, and included a battalion of German tanks. On 8 September 1943, the 18º Reggimento bersaglieri joined the formation in Rome and fought German units when the fascist units did not. The XIX Battaglione carri, equipped with M15/42 tanks and Semovente 75/34 self-propelled guns, did not get to Rome in time to participate.

An M15/42 medium tank on parade in Genoa, Italy, on 2 June 1951. Roughly 200 M15/42s survived World War II and remained in Italian Army service into the 1950s. (De Agostini Picture Library/Getty Images)

BIBLIOGRAPHY

Blumberg, A. (2018). 'WWII Tanks: Italy's Failed Iterations.' Available online at warfarehistorynetwork.com/article/wwii-tanks-italys-failed-iterations (accessed 10 November 2023).

Campini, D. (2015a). *El Alamein i carri della Littorio.* Zanica: Soldiershop Publishing.

Campini, D. (2015b). *Ferrea Mole Ferreo Cuore.* Zanica: Soldiershop Publishing.

Cappellano, F. & Battistelli, P.P. (2012). *Italian Medium Tanks 1939–45.* New Vanguard 195. Oxford: Osprey Publishing.

Cristini, L. (2022). *Italian Medium Tank M13-40, M14-41 & M15-42.* Zanica: Soldiershop Publishing.

Fletcher, D. (1995). *Crusader and Covenanter Cruiser Tanks 1939–45.* New Vanguard 14. Oxford: Osprey Publishing.

Jentz, T.L. (1998). *Tank Combat in North Africa.* Atglen, PA: Schiffer.

Knight, P.M. (2015). *A15 Cruiser Mk. VI Crusader Tank: A Technical History.* Lexington, KY: Black Prince.

Montanari, M. (2007). *The Three Battles of El Alamein.* Rome: Stato Maggiore Dell'Esercito.

Pitman, S. (1950). *Second Royal Gloucestershire Hussars.* London: St Catherine Press.

Rebora, A. (2021). *La divisione Ariete a Bir El Gobi.* Lucca: Tralerighe libri.

Riccio, R. & Afiero, M. (2022). *Luck was Lacking but Valour was Not: The Italian Army in North Africa, 1940–43.* Warwick: Helion.

The remains of a Crusader tank on the El Alamein battlefield, 29 May 1976. (The People/Mirrorpix/Mirrorpix via Getty Images)

INDEX